WHAT TO DO *when you don't know* WHAT TO DO

Neil Eskelin

WHAT TO DO WHEN YOU
DON'T KNOW WHAT TO DO

ISBN 0-9641058-5-3

Published by

WESTERN FRONT, LTD.
416 Paseo Del Mar
Palos Verdes, CA 90274

Printed in the United States of America.

OTHER BOOKS BY NEIL ESKELIN

YES YES LIVING IN A NO NO WORLD

THE TWENTY-FOUR HOUR TURN-AROUND

101 PROMISES WORTH KEEPING

POWERFUL PRINCIPLES
FOR PERSONAL GROWTH
(AUDIO/VIDEO)

LEADERS ARE LOVERS

Contents

Introduction

"Do you have just a moment?" a man in his early forties asked after I had finished a leadership seminar in Florida. His name was Robert.

"Certainly," I responded, and we began to talk.

"I've got some big decisions to make and I need your advice," he stated as he gave me a thumb-nail sketch of the dilemma he was facing.

After our brief meeting, as I was driving to the airport, I thought about Robert's quandary. His immediate crisis concerned his career. In reality, however, almost every aspect of his life would be affected by the choices he was about to make — his family, his finances and his future.

During the flight I tried to get a few minutes rest but all I could think of was the man who was wrestling with indecision. Then, as if a light had suddenly been switched on, it suddenly dawned on me that Robert's plight was no different than that of hundreds of people who had previously asked for my advice. The circumstances are always unique, but the basic question is the same: "I'm facing a decision. What should I do?"

An Uncertain Future

From Wall Street to the west coast, and in foreign nations,

I have talked with countless people who were at a crossroads — trapped in a valley of indecision, engulfed by circumstances or troubled about tomorrow. They ask:

"Where should I turn for help?"

"How can I know what I *really* should be doing?"

"What steps should I take to rebuild my life?"

"How can I overcome negative influences of my past?"

I have met those who are under great stress because of the pressure of finances, who feel hopeless because of a medical diagnosis, or who are emotionally drained because of a difficult relationship. Uncertainty is not bound by age.

I've talked with young people attempting to make sense out of life's choices and senior citizens searching for meaningful activity.

Looking For Answers

This book is not only for those whose employment has suddenly ceased or whose marriage has crumbled, but for the person who has that restless, uncertain feeling and says, "I know there is something far better I should be doing with my life."

On these pages you will discover:

- How to escape from confusion and uncertainty.
- What to do before making a fresh start.
- How to find a vision that will lift your life.
- The secrets of uncovering your hidden gifts and talents.
- What to say when you talk to yourself.
- How to seize control of your future.
- How to make failure impossible.
- How to give help and direction to those you love.

It is my desire that you will turn to these pages again and again for personal inspiration and guidance. I also pray that this information will be a valuable resource when you are reaching out to someone whose life is at a standstill.

"Destiny is not a matter of chance, it is a matter of choice," observed William Jennings Bryan. "It is not a thing to be waited for, it is a thing to be achieved."

Dreaming great dreams and thinking positive thoughts are important but, as you will see, they are only starting points. This volume is not about wishing or hoping, but about specific actions you can take to move from confusion to confidence — from apprehension to achievement.

Most important, I believe you will find the answer to *what to do when you don't know what to do.*

1

Help! I Don't Know What to Do!

"We are always getting ready
to live, but never living."
— Emerson

A second grade teacher asked her students to write a little essay about their mother or father. "Write anything you want," she told her students.

Here is what a little boy wrote about his father:

"My dad can climb the highest mountain.
My dad can fly the fastest jet.
My dad can beat the meanest tiger.
But most of the time he just carries out the garbage."

The second-grader *wished* he had a father who could accomplish the impossible, but instead he saw a dad stuck in the routine of life.

We are all born into a world that is filled with great

promise. As children we believe we can attain the status of "Superman" and soar to the skies. Unfortunately, something happens on our journey to rob us of that hope and steal our vision of tomorrow.

I would like to tell you that most people are conditioned to succeed, but that is far from the truth. Instead, we are programmed to fail.

Psychologists tell us that a typical child is told "No," an average of fifteen times every day while growing up. That amounts to 100,000 negative messages during the first eighteen years of our life.

How many "Yes" messages do we hear? Sadly, the number is far too small.

By the time we reach the age of six, eighty percent of our personality and outlook on life is developed. Day after day, layer upon layer, our self-image is permanently etched.

Should we be surprised when behaviorists tell us that in the average person, as much as seventy percent of everything we think about is negative or counterproductive? This is a result of being bombarded with the bad, not the good.

In a world that is changing faster than the hands on a clock, people everywhere are not only uncertain, they are paralyzed by fear and anxiety. You only have to glance at the explosion of technology to know that if you fall one step behind the parade may pass you by.

Until the advent of the printing press we lived in an "oral" world where history was spoken. Then came the "linear" world of reading. Now children no longer read left to right, they follow a computer screen from top to bottom and are guided by icons and graphics in our new "symbolic" world.

The universe is changing, and so must we. As the Greek philosopher Hercalitus observed long ago, "You cannot step twice into the same river, for other waters are continually flowing in."

What has happened in this innovative age? Many have simply given up.

Already Dead?

Recently, two women knocked on my door and handed me a little religious pamphlet with the title, *Millions Now Living Will Never Die.*

I smiled and commented, "I think you should change the headline."

"What do you mean?" one responded.

"It should say, 'Millions now living are already dead!'"

I was serious. I meet people every day who are lifeless. There is no sparkle in their eye and no grip in their handshake. For all practical purposes they have given up.

Instead of living, millions of people *watch* life as it goes by. I doubt I will ever be able to comprehend why someone would tune in to a fishing show on a beautiful summer day instead of heading for the nearest lake. If the Bible were being written today there would probably be a verse that says, "Without a television the people perish."

Going in Circles

When I was a boy I loved to hear my father tell me what it was like growing up in the Upper Peninsula of Michigan. That is where his family immigrated from Finland to work in the copper mines.

There was one story I always asked my dad to repeat. "Every winter," he recalled, "my friends and I went to the top of a very high hill and dug a tunnel in the snow." The twelve and thirteen year old boys began by digging an entrance that was like a chute that went straight down a few feet. "Then we dug a circle around the top of the hill."

Their next step was to persuade some young boys about five or six years old to join them. "We would drop them into the opening and yell "Keep to the left! Keep to the left!"

My dad related how the little boys would crawl around that tunnel in a circle until, exhausted, they would begin to cry. Responding to their wails, the older boys would yell, "Go to the right."

What the unsuspecting youngsters didn't know was that the older boys had dug one final tunnel. It came down the side of the steep hill. "When we yelled for the crying boys to go to the right we would run to the bottom of hill and laugh as they came flying out into the sunshine."

Many people are like those boys in that tunnel — going around in circles.

A man in Los Angeles asked his employer why three other people were promoted past him. He said, "Sir, I just don't understand. I have twenty years of experience in this job."

His employer gave him a reply that really jolted him. "I

hate to tell you this," he explained, "but you really don't have twenty years of experience. You have *one* year of experience twenty times. You've been doing things the same old way since the day you started."

There are times in our life when it is imperative that we change our course and move in a new direction. Our very survival may be at stake.

What Did I Really Want?

I can clearly remember a time in my life when my future seemed like a road sign that read, "Dead End." At the age of twenty-three I had completed two college degrees and had some work experience, but I was restless and unfulfilled.

One sleepless night I had a serious talk with myself. I asked dozens of questions about my future. What did I really want to do? I pondered,

"If there were no barriers in my life and I could do absolutely anything I wanted, what would it be?"

The answer seemed rather improbable. I was young and single and said to myself, "I would like to travel the world and get paid for it — I'd even like to be a professional speaker and tell people about my experiences."

It is amazing how a dominating thought can become a powerful magnet so strong that every thought and action is attracted toward it.

From that moment forward, I began to save every dollar I could for a trip to Africa. I bought a detailed map of the dark continent and began to carefully plan my journey. Even more, I announced my plans and started making contacts with people I would visit on the trip.

There was one question, however, that loomed rather large. What would I do when I returned. How could I realistically turn my experiences into a livelihood?

One week before the time of my flight I went to New York City with one objective. I wanted to explore every possibility of developing a program on Africa and presenting it to the public.

Where would I begin? Who would I contact? I walked into the lobby of a hotel near Central Park and headed for the telephones. I opened the Yellow Pages and looked under "Lecture and Entertainment Bureaus." The list was long — at least forty booking agencies.

Local calls were only ten cents. I went to the cashier armed with four one-dollar bills and said, "I need as many dimes as you can spare."

Then I walked over to a pay phone and paused for a moment. "Lord," I said, "I going to really need your help today!" Then I began to feed the phone.

"Hello. My name is Neil Eskelin. I'm on my way to Africa to gather material for a program on that part of the world. Do you have any openings for a speaker on this topic?"

"Thanks for your call," the secretary would politely say, "but I don't think we'd be interested."

More then thirty dimes later, the response was still the same. I had not heard one word of encouragement. "Perhaps I should I give up this crazy idea?" I thought.

Just as I was about to walk away from the pay phone, I decided to redial the number of an agency I had tried to reach three times. Previously there had always a busy signal, but this time someone answered.

"Hello. This is Neil Eskelin — " and I began my well-rehearsed pitch.

The woman on the phone introduced herself as the manager of the agency and said, "Could you come over to my office today? I need to talk with you."

Forty-five minutes later I was standing in the lobby of a small lecture bureau near Columbus Circle. The smiling director exclaimed, "You won't believe this, but just a few minutes before you called, I had a message from a school assembly agency that one of their programs for this year had been canceled. They need a replacement immediately. You would be doing a tour of 400 schools starting in September. Are you interested?"

Minutes later I was on the phone with the Director of Supervised Study at North Dakota State University. We discussed the details of the program, "Inside Africa" I would prepare and present under their sponsorship.

What did I do when I didn't know what to do?

I followed my heart. I went to a city I did not know, called people I had never met, and literally traveled to Timbuktu.

What happened? The tour through the snows of the Dakotas opened doors I thought I would never enter. The next summer I found myself as the opening night speaker to an audience of 3000 at the annual convention of the International Platform Association. They named me to the Board of Governors with Lowell Thomas and Art Buchwald and I was signed for several years of national speaking tours — from the Knife and Fork Clubs to colleges and universities.

If you are bewildered by the future, you are in great company. We have all been there. There is a time, however, when we must come face to face with our confusion.

On the pages that follow you will be asked to make some important decisions. I believe they will be the first steps of an exciting new adventure.

2

Which Road Should I Take?

"Two roads diverged in a wood and I,
I took the one less traveled by.
And that has made all the difference."
— Robert Frost

A man was driving through the Black Hills of South Dakota, when suddenly he found himself in the middle of a blinding snowstorm. As he came to a small town he was relieved to see a snowplow ahead of him. He kept as close to the vehicle as possible while it was cleaning the pavement. The snow was accumulating so fast he could hardly see the machine.

A few minutes later the plow stopped and the operator got out and walked over to the car. "Mister, where are you headed?" the driver asked.

"I'm on my way to Mount Rushmore," the man responded.

"Well, you'll never get there following me. I'm plowing

out this parking lot."

Many go through life believing they can reach their destination by playing "follow the leader." They look for someone who is stronger, smarter, or more successful than themselves and attempt to tag along. The strategy almost always backfires.

A victory is hollow unless it is your victory — based on the personal choices you have made.

I have a small book in my library that carries a great message. The book is entitled *Your Greatest Power* and was written by J. Martin Kohe. In this fascinating volume, Kohe writes, "You are the possessor of a great and wonderful power. This power, when properly applied, will bring confidence instead of timidity, calmness instead of confusion, poise instead of restlessness, and peace of mind in place of heartache. What is your greatest power? The power to choose."

Every day we make hundreds of choices. We choose what radio station we will listen to, what restaurant we will visit for lunch, what brand of toothpaste we will buy, whether we will repeat the latest gossip, how much we will give to our church, and the list goes on.

Why is it that people spend so little time preparing for the big choices of life that will determine their future? How can a person who spends several years in college preparing for a career suddenly accept the first opportunity that comes in their path — an occupation that often bears no resemblance to their personal goals or training?

Stop for a moment and ask yourself this question: "Who is in charge of my life? Am I only reacting to circumstances, or am I truly making decisions?"

During the past several years I have heard many people try to explain their personal failures. Here just a few examples.

- "It's totally out of my control. Whatever will be will be."
- "I guess I'm a bad person since so many bad things happen to me."
- Change is too tough. I'm not sure I have the will power.
- "The devil must not like me. He keeps messing up my life."
- "Nobody wants to help me and I certainly can't succeed on my own."

Self-criticism is a barrier to change that must be removed. As you will see, you already possess the talents and qualities necessary for achievement. But what about your greatest power — the power to choose? Are you exercising it in the big issues of life?

The Danger of Resistance

Change is not something to be feared, but to be embraced as part of your permanent lifestyle.

To some, however, even minor change can produce major rebellion. The office manager of a large Wall Street brokerage firm said, "I am constantly surprised at how some people go into hysterics if someone alters their working environment. I've seen grown men throw temper tantrums when they are told to relocate their office."

The unemployment lines are crowded with people who say, "I refuse to change." In many cases it is because people fail to adapt to new technology.

You only need to take a quick glance at our society to realize that with every passing year the life cycles of new products are becoming shorter and shorter. Now, almost from the day a new consumer product is created, a team from research and development is working around the clock on its replacement.

John F. Kennedy said, "Change is the law of life. And those who look only to the past or the present are certain to miss the future."

Here is the message of the president of a computer company. He stated, "Our merchandise is designed to last only nine or ten months." Then he added:

"If we don't have a 'new update' or introduce something that includes a major change, the market will pass us by. We'll be history."

A group of executives asked individuals why they weren't

responding to directives to adopt new procedures. Here are the answers they gave.

"That's the way we were taught to do it around here."

"I didn't have time to read the new guidelines."

"I thought someone else would be able to finish the job."

"I didn't think it was that important."

"No one ever really explained the new process to me."

In today's climate, comments like these are rarely tolerated. As Everett M. Dirksen observed, "Life is not a static thing. The only people who do not change their minds are incompetents in asylums, who can't, and those in cemeteries."

What lessons should we learn about change? Here are ten important things to remember about choice and personal transformation.

1. You were created with "transforming" abilities.

The same God who made flowers that would bloom in the spring and seas that would rise and fall with the tides, also made you. Just as our physical bodies grow and become renewed, our thoughts and behavior must also be transformed. In Jeremiah 7, here is what God told the prophet, "If you really change your ways and your actions . . . I will let you live in this place."

2. Become willing to change.

Transformation should not be something that happens *to* us, but a change we initiate. If we can learn to reprogram our computer, why can't we reprogram ourselves? Columnist Sidney Harris states, "Our dilemma is that we hate change and love it at the same time; what we want is for things to remain the same but get better."

3. Only by learning from small choices can you successfully make bigger ones.

Don't allow the minor decisions you make every day to become so automatic you ignore what is taking place. Whether buying a magazine at the news stand or selecting the kind of account to open at your bank, stop for a moment and reflect on what you are learning from the experience.

4. Be flexible, not rigid.

People who become dogmatic and give "Yes" or "No" answers to every question often paint themselves in a corner from which there is no escape. Always leave the door ajar for change. Give yourself some breathing room to look at issues in a creative way.

5. Clear the emotional barriers of your past.

Don't allow yourself to make choices based on remorse, guilt, hate or anger. If your decision is motivated by "trying to get even," you are dealing with a double-edged sword that will cause more harm to you than to the person who is your target.

Examine your hidden motives. For example, you can't be positive if you hate positive people. You will never have wealth if you hate wealthy people.

6. Don't allow yesterday's problems to build and multiply.

Ignoring the difficulties of your past won't cause them to disappear. Tackle every question head-on. If your mind and heart are crowded with unresolved issues, there is no room for personal growth.

7. After you learn the lesson, bury the experience.

The only question you need to ask from a past failure is, "What did I learn from the incident or encounter?" When that lesson is clear, mentally and symbolically hold a funeral service for the issue. If God can forgive and forget, so can we.

8. Minimize the power of external influences.

External influences — peer pressure, the media, social and political issues — are minor compared to the decisions we make internally. Often, we use the sway of our environment as an excuse for behavior, but it is what we think that matters most.

9. Guidance comes only to things that are in motion.

When you have made a decision, don't just stand there. Start moving forward. It's almost impossible to balance a stationary bicycle, but the task becomes almost effortless when you start moving.

10. The power to choose is meaningless unless you choose.

A skilled craftsman may have the best tools in the world, but unless he takes them in his hand and begins to work, there will be no art. That's how it is with choice. Only when we exercise our power will we see the results.

Remember:

You *choose* to believe in yourself.
You *choose* to make your own decisions.
You *choose* to stop making excuses.

You *choose* to accept responsibility for your actions.
You *choose* to have faith and belief.
You *choose* to do what is right.
You *choose* to change.

3

Target Your Talent

"Men habitually use only a small part
of the powers they actually possess."
— William James

What is the shortest path to success? It is found in this one phrase: Build on your strength, not your weakness.

One of the great flaws of human nature is that we spend tremendous amounts of time and energy trying to balance our skill bank. If we have a natural talent we accept it and spend very little time on its nourishment and improvement. Instead we concentrate on our deficiencies — trying desperately to find remedies and cures.

"Oh, I already know how to do that," a college student told me when he was about to choose an elective in art — an area in which he was especially gifted. He wanted a course in applied economics. "I really need to know more about that."

Someone defined a PhD as a person who knows more and more about less and less. There are great benefits, however, to such an approach.

If I were to offer you my best advice, I would first want

to know, "In what topic do you have exceptional knowledge? And "What is the greatest talent you possess?"

That is your starting point. From that juncture your objective should be to take your gift to the highest possible level of proficiency.

I remember the time I taught public speaking at the college level. Most students would spend hours in the library "boning up" on a subject that was totally new to them. They would stand before the class and become so nervous their note cards would began to shake and their voice would quiver.

I told the class, "Don't talk about what you *don't* know, present what you know best." Then I explained,

"You are already the world's greatest authority on one topic. You know more about what has happened to you than any person on earth."

It is true. When you speak from personal experience you exude more self-confidence and authority than you realize. It is reflected in the response of the audience. They are usually totally captivated by your personal narrative.

Are you aware of your personal talents? Writer Robert Half says, "There is something that is much more scarce, something rarer than ability. It is the ability to recognize ability."

Don't Bury Your Talent

Invest in your natural gifts wisely. Use what you *have* not what you *don't* have.

I often reflect on the biblical story of the talents. A talent was an ancient unit of money, and the account is a parallel to individual ability.

The parable opens with the master of a wealthy estate preparing for a journey into a far country. Prior to his departure, he entrusted a portion of his wealth to three of his servants. To one he gave five talents. To the second servant he gave two talents. The third servant received one talent. Each was instructed to use what they had been given.

About a year later, the master returned and called together his servants to see how they had done. The servant who was given five talents had invested wisely and now possessed ten talents.

The master said, "Well done, thou good and faithful servant. Because you have been faithful with what you have, I will give you more."

The second servant also used what had been given to him and the master was likewise pleased with his efforts.

Can you imagine how the third servant must have felt? The master inquired how he had done. "You only gave me one talent," responded the servant," and I was very careful not to misuse it. In fact, I put it in a safe place while you were gone. Here it is — as good as new"

The master was outraged. "Thou wicked and slothful servant! How dare you not wisely use what I gave you." He then took the talent and gave it to the servant who had ten.

The third servant reminds me of those who complain, "Everybody else gets all the breaks."

Here is the message of the master: "Don't bury your

talent. Take what you have and use it. What you originally possess will be multiplied again and again."

Storing our talents in a safe place or keeping them buried can result in the loss of the very thing we are trying to protect.

No matter what abilities you possess, use them to their fullest. Invest them wisely in people, projects, and activities, and you will find they will multiply. It is an irrevocable law: "What you sow, that will you also reap."

Dave's Way

Dave Thomas, the founder of Wendy's, had a difficult childhood that give him the conviction and determination to succeed. He was adopted, but lost his mother when he was five. After her death, his adoptive father married three more times and moved the family frequently. When he was twelve, Dave got his first job and quit school after the tenth grade to work full-time in the restaurant business.

He worked his way up from a busboy in a family restaurant to being the manager of four failing Kentucky Fried Chicken franchises. The late founder of KFC, Colonel Harland Sanders, became Thomas's mentor and taught him how to promote a business.

Dave absorbed the lessons of Sanders like a sponge. Before long he had revitalized the Kentucky Fried Chicken franchises from red ink to black — and he was made a partner in those businesses. By the age of thirty-five he had the capital to open his first Wendy's. It was 1969.

Today, Thomas has removed himself from most of the operational responsibilities. In his book, *Dave's Way,* he admits to being a cheerleader and marketer, but not effective with day-to-day details. He travels the country, in between doing commercials, to insure quality control and to motivate Wendy's employees.

Dave Thomas took a hard look at his abilities and talents. He placed himself in a position that would capitalize on his strengths — doing what he does best. That's what makes him the inspiration behind Wendy's success.

I asked someone recently, "When is the last time you took an aptitude test?"

"Oh, I think I took one in high school, but the guidance counselor didn't tell me the results."

Perhaps it is time to take such a test again and ask yourself, "Am I doing what is right for me? Are my talents being aimed in the right direction?"

Many people are surprised at how quickly they can reach new levels when they concentrate on their abilities.

Spending five minutes a day for five years on one topic will place you in the top one percent in any given field of study.

Where Do I Begin?

Zig Ziglar observed, "I've read a lot of birth announcements. They always indicated that the newborn was either a boy or a girl. Yet I have never read of the arrival of a doctor, a salesperson, accountant, or member of any other profession."

Parents can do a lot of wishing and day-dreaming about the future of their children. They can provide the best environment, pay for the best education, and introduce them to people who have the right connections. But does that guarantee success? Not at all. It may improve the odds, but ultimate achievement will eventually rest entirely on the shoulders of the child.

With so many choices, opportunities, and directions available, some may ask, "Where do I begin? What's the first step?"

Have you ever looked at a store directory at the entrance to a large shopping mall? There is usually a map to help you get oriented. On it you'll find a highlighted spot with these words: "You Are Here."

What do most people think about when they want to make a fresh start? "Oh, I think I'll move to another part of the country." Or, "I feel I could do much better if I signed on with another company."

The problem with that premise is this:

Changing locations without changing yourself is like parking a rusty car in a new garage. The atmosphere may be different but inside, it's still the same.

Friend, I can tell you the grass is not greener on the other side of the world. A different job, a different home, and even a different partner will not resolve the problem. Our transformation can only begin when we examine the inside.

Behavioral scientists know that we have to deal with what *is* before we can adequately face future possibilities. Failure to deal with reality is the reason people make so little progress.

The Best Path

Several years ago, my wife and I sat spellbound during a concert by the famed violinist, Itzhak Perlman. He has thrilled audiences around the globe. The fact that he is handicapped becomes a minor point when you are lost in the magic of his talent.

Perlman was asked about his early years and he explained, "I had a fairly normal childhood, considering two rather unusual elements. I had polio and walked with crutches, and I practiced the violin two or three hours a day." Then he added, "Actually, spending so much time with the violin was harder to explain than my crutches."

Are you doing everything in your power to develop the talent you have been granted? Every day schedule time to sharpen your God-given skills.

Thomas Wolfe, in his book, *The Web and the Rock,* wrote "If we have a talent and cannot use it, we have failed. If we have a talent and use only *half* of it, we have *partly* failed. If we have a talent and learn somehow to use *all* of it, we have gloriously succeeded, and won a satisfaction and a triumph few individuals ever know."

What path should you take? The answer is easy. Take the road that is already paved with your talents, your experience, and the throbbing of your heart. Don't strike out on a new course in an arena you don't understand.

Target your talent. Build on it and watch it unfold into something beautiful.

4

Don't Wake Me, I'm Dreaming!

"It man be those who
do most, dream most."
— Stephen Leacock

I remember driving across the Arizona desert and seeing what looked like a small dot on the horizon. I immediately guessed that it was a large billboard several miles ahead. The closer I came to the sign, the larger it loomed. And when I finally passed it, the billboard was bigger than life.

That's how it is with our dreams. What begins as a distant dot suddenly becomes a towering reality as we move toward it.

When you first begin to form a picture of your future it may seem hazy, even out of focus. But the longer you think about it the more vivid and substantial it becomes. Eventually, we began to attach meaning to our vision and it becomes concrete and tangible. As Johathan Swift wrote, "Vision is the art of seeing things invisible."

When you finally zero in on the central, overriding dream of your life, it seems there is nothing — absolutely nothing — that will keep you from attaining it. If someone erects a blockade you won't be alarmed. You will go around it, under it, or over it to reach your objective.

There's Only One "It"

If you have ever raised a child you know how difficult it can sometimes be for the infant to obey orders. For example, if the doctor prescribes that you give a baby some medication, you can try with all your might to have the child swallow that pill, but it won't always happen.

Let me share a secret with you. It is the simplest thing in the world to get a toddler to swallow a pill. All you need to do is place the capsule in the middle of the floor and walk out of the room. The baby will crawl to the pill and swallow it instantly. Why? Because the child found "it."

Have you found the "it" for your life? Have the curtains of your mind parted so that you can view the full picture that includes the details of your future?

Visualization works. Perhaps you have closed your eyes and imagined that you were standing on the top of a mountain, looking over a wide panorama. Suddenly you are thinking higher thoughts and expanding your universe.

How vital is dreaming? Albert Einstein stated that "Imagination is more important than knowledge, for knowledge is limited to all we now know and understand, while imagination embraces the entire world, and all there ever *will* be to know and understand."

The power of the mind God has blessed you with is awesome. We have the ability to store up to 100 billion — not million, but *billion* — pieces of information and it is there for our retrieval. The brain, however, has been described as a muscle that must be exercised. The "use it or lose it" law applies.

Medical science has proven that the thoughts we place in our mind have extraordinary power. They can raise or lower our body temperature, relax our muscles or produce nervous energy.

Our mind — in response to our thoughts — can open or close our arteries and raise or lower our pulse rate.

Charles Swindol, in his book *Living Beyond Mediocrity,* said, "I have in mind the ability to see above and beyond the majority. I am reminded of the eagle, which has eight times as many visual cells per cubic centimeter than does a human. This translates into rather astounding abilities. For example, flying at 600 feet elevation, an eagle can spot an object the size of a dime moving through six-inch grass. The same creature can see three-inch fish jumping in a lake five miles away." Says Swindoll, "Eagle-like people can envision what most would miss. Visionary people see beyond the hum-drum of everyday activities into future possibilities."

A New You

I remember listening to a young lady by the name of Norma. She told her story of running with violent youth gangs through the dark streets of Toronto. She was involved in everything from mugging individuals to robbing stores. After a dramatic spiritual conversion, Norma returned to her old neighborhood and invited her former friends to come to a church to hear her speak.

At the conclusion of her "sinner to saint" story, several of her earlier partners in crime questioned her.

"But what about the time we beat that elderly woman and stole her purse?" one young man asked.

"That wasn't me," she replied. "That was the old Norma. You are looking at a brand new person" — and she quoted chapter and verse that says "If anyone is in Christ, he is a new creation; the old has gone, the new has come!"

A transformation can become so complete that the negatives of the past can be viewed as belonging to someone else - not you.

The Power of Your Mind's Eye

In his book, *Psycho-Cybernetics,* Dr. Maxwell Maltz tells of an experiment that showed how mental practice can actually improve our skills. The test involved the ability to sink basketball free throws. Maltz says that "One group of students actually practiced throwing the ball every day for twenty days." Their efforts were recorded on the first and last day.

A second group, that was also tested on the first and last day, engaged in no sort of practice between their tests.

A third group was scored on the first day, then spent 20 minutes every day "imagining" that they were throwing the ball at the basket. When they missed they would imagine that they corrected their aim accordingly.

Here's what the results showed. The first group, which actually practiced twenty minutes a day, improved their scoring ability by twenty-four percent. The second group, which had no sort of practice, showed no improvement. The third group, who practiced only in their imagination, improved in scoring twenty-three percent!

When you change your mind's eye, you see things differently with your physical eye. Soon the view from the inside becomes manifest in the way you walk, the words you speak, and the manner in which people respond to you.

Arnold Schwarzenegger won the title of Mr. Universe seven times. But he didn't keep his title by only pumping iron. As part of his workout routine, he would frequently go into the corner of the gym and visualize himself winning the title again.

Jack Nicklaus, the great professional golfer, explained his imaging technique. He said, "First I 'see' the ball where I want it to finish — nice and white and sitting up high on the bright green grass. Then the scene quickly changes, and I 'see' the ball going there; its path, trajectory and shape, even its behavior on landing. Then," says Nicklaus, "there's a sort of fade-out, and the next scene shows me making the kind of swing that will turn the previous images into reality."

I recall hearing the story of a prisoner of war who spent his years of solitary confinement playing golf — on the courses of his mind. When he was released and returned to California, one of his first desires was to head for the nearest golfing facility. He was totally shocked at how his game had improved. Without question, his imagination had greatly enhanced his physical skills.

Ideas have amazing strength.

Albert Schweitzer, the great doctor who gave his life to the people of Africa, observed that "The power of an idea is incalculable." He observed,

"We see no power in a drop of water, but just let it get into a crack in the rock and be turned to ice, and it splits the rock. When it is turned into steam, it drives the pistons of the most powerful engines."

As Schweitzer stated, "Something has happened to it which makes active and effective the power that is latent in it."

David Schwartz, in his book, *The Magic of Thinking Success,* says, "Wishing is different from dreaming. Wishing is passive and inactive. Wishing is an idle pastime with no brains or effort behind it. But dreaming is backed up with an action plan to produce results."

A Giant Chart

In Oklahoma I was invited to speak at a banquet for a small non-profit corporation. The president of the project took me to his office and I couldn't help but notice that one entire wall was covered with a huge organizational chart. There were more than one hundred "boxes" with the titles of secretaries, directors and vice presidents.

"I didn't realize you had this many employees," I commented.

"We don't," the man smiled. "Those are the positions we *will* have when we get this thing running at full speed."

It was obvious the man had a vision.

Several years ago I read a short sentence that I couldn't get out of my mind. It said, "What motivates people, motivates people."

At first I thought, "How silly." But the more I pondered the statement, the more it made sense. If we want to motivate people we learn exactly what they want and offer them a way to obtain it. But what about you? What is your motivation? Is it the dream of seeing every square on an organizational chart become a reality? Is it being able to retire in the home you envision?

Tell me your dream and I'll instantly know what

motivates you. Without a vision there is only vacuum and void.

A word of warning: Beware of low aim. Keep your thoughts on your highest dream and never lower your sights. Develop the patience to keep moving up the steady incline toward your target.

Why do so many people allow their ideals for tomorrow to be shelved? They are swallowed up by the desire to be accepted by their circle of friends and to survive in their current work environment. Personal ambitions and plans are put aside and often destroyed.

Dream on! Hold tightly to the vision that will not only lift your life, but will inspire those around you.

5

How High Can I Really Climb?

"A man's conquest of himself
dwarfs the ascent of Everest."
— Eli J. Schiefer

It's time for an inventory.

If the truth about your abilities were revealed, what would you learn? Research shows that three out of every four people are best suited for working with others rather than working alone. What about you? Have you identified the one area of life where you plan to shine like a sparkling diamond?

Is your objective realistic?

You can talk to any psychologist and learn that people who plan to fail choose goals that are totally out of reach. From the first moment they discuss their dream, they know in their heart of hearts there is no chance for its fulfillment.

On the other hand, winners select a target that is not only achievable, but they also choose a series of interim goals that will provide the satisfaction of continual success along the way.

What about your values? Have you defined them? Knowing what makes you tick is not just an academic exercise. Rather, it is a down-to-earth action toward realizing fulfillment in life. Noted psychologist Carl Rogers said, "Clarifying your values is the first step toward a richer, fuller, more productive life."

To better understand the issues of character and integrity ask yourself:

What do I believe in?
What are my guiding principles?
What governs my thoughts and actions?
What do I stand for?
What puts meaning and purpose in my existence?
What qualities are important if I am to be a complete person?

The Market Price

If your life could be traded on the stock market what would the equity be worth? Would the price per share be escalating or plummeting?

The value of everything is constantly changing so rapidly that grocery stores no longer print the price of the product on the merchandise. Instead it is inserted on a bar code that can be changed as often as necessary to meet the competition, adjust for inflation, or be placed on sale. John Barth wrote, "Nothing is intrinsically valuable; the value of everything is attributed to it, assigned to it from outside the thing itself, by people."

What can you do to increase your self-worth? It begins when we increase our self-perception. That sends a clear message to the world that we have faith, confidence and belief in the mission of our life.

Don't sell yourself short. As the great American patriot, Thomas Paine, stated, "What we obtain too cheap, we esteem too lightly; it is dearness only that gives everything its value."

Have you learned to love yourself? I'm not talking about an inflated ego, arrogance or conceit. If you cannot identify your attractive qualities, how do you expect others to recognize them?

Your Weakest Spot

Since you know yourself better than anyone else, perhaps you have already identified what you consider to be a weak spot in your character or personality. It may give you apprehension. Don't worry. It's perfectly normal. Helen Keller stated,

"All uncertainty is fruitful — so long as it is accompanied by the wish to understand."

If you have read Greek mythology, you know that Achilles was a great warrior. The story is told that his mother, wanting to make her infant son invulnerable to attack, dipped him in the river Styx.

The waters of the river were considered magical and they covered every part of the boy except Achilles' heel — that is where the mother held him.

Later in life, he became a great warrior and conquered all

of his enemies. His chief adversary, Paris, hit him with an arrow in his only spot of weakness; his heel.

What is your Achilles' heel? Instead of making it your point of failure, use the knowledge to grow and mature.

A flaw can make room for an infection that spreads to other parts of your character.

Don't give your weakness more prominence than it deserves. When you focus on faults you give them unnecessary influence.

You can identify your Achilles' heel by asking yourself, "I am confident of my abilities, except for . . ." Or, "I could be more successful if it were not for . . ."

There is no such thing as a perfect situation. Even when you reach for the stars, there may be ominous clouds on your horizon.

Neil Armstrong, the first man to walk on the moon, was asked if he was nervous contemplating his trip into space. "Who wouldn't be," he responded. "There I was sitting on top of 9,999 parts and bits — each of which had been made by the lowest bidder."

Build a Wide Foundation

How high can you really climb? The answer depends on the width and depth of your foundation.

When you were a child, you probably tried to see how tall you could build a tower of dominos or tin cans before they came crashing down.

What you quickly learned was this: when there is only one item at the base, you cannot build much of a tower. But look what happens when *several* pieces form the base of your column. In physics there is a rule that says: *the wider the foundation the higher the structure.*

That axiom is also a basic principle of personal development. We build our foundation by the knowledge we obtain and the people with whom we associate.

Be honest and ask yourself, "What kind of people are attracted to me?"

I remember seeing a cartoon of two hippopotami kissing each other. The caption read, "What you like depends on what you are used to."

A college administrator told me about an observation he made about students. He said, "I can stand in the cafeteria on the day freshmen students arrive and watch the future trouble-makers gather together as if pulled by some unseen force. Student leaders form their alliances immediately, too," he observed. Like attracts like.

Have you ever noticed that angry people attract those who are angry just as positive people surround themselves with those who are optimistic?

When we choose who *we* are, we are in the best position to determine who will help us build our foundation.

Your Information Explosion

In addition to the people with whom we associate, our

foundation is fortified by the information we acquire. It has been said that everybody feeds their bodies, but only successful people nourish their minds.

A friend of mine who is the dean of a graduate school told me his favorite question to prospective students is this: "What books have you read in the past few weeks?"

The answer to that inquiry tells him more about the student than almost any other indicator.

If someone asked you the same question, would you be proud of your answer, or embarrassed?

There is an old epigram that states,

"The person who can read and doesn't has no advantage over the person who can't read."

Reading is not a luxury for people who have nothing better to do. It is a life-enhancing necessity. As Henry Ford said, "Anyone who stops learning is old, whether at twenty or eighty. Anyone who keeps learning stays young."

Some people think that when they earn a college degree, they possess all the knowledge they need for life. Far from it. Harry Truman observed, "The only things worth learning are the things you learn after you know it all."

I'm a great proponent of self-help books because they develop life skills and keep the flame of hope and expectation burning bright. They are the building blocks that will help us achieve our potential. Psychologist Albert Maslow says, "If you deliberately plan to be less than you are capable of being, then I warn you that you'll be unhappy for the rest of your life."

What's amazing about reading motivational volumes is that the contents always seem original and fresh — even if you have read the same book before. Why is that the case?

One day, you'll pick up one of Napoleon Hill's books and say, "I never saw that before." The reason it seems new is because of the way *you* have changed. The growth you've experienced has prepared you to apply concepts and ideas you were not ready for last year, or the year before.

There is another way you can build your storehouse of knowledge — by listening.

How many miles do you put on your automobile each year? If you drive 10,000 miles you are spending at least two hundred hours behind the wheel.

Think for a moment about how productive those hours would be if you were listening to self-help materials. The explosion of books-on-tape and audio libraries makes this kind of information available almost everywhere.

The next time you are planning a journey, after you calculate the miles, say "This is a six tape trip" and choose the information you will hear. As writer Thomas Aldrich states, "A man is known by the company his mind keeps."

Sharpen Your Skills

People with great imaginations almost always have a wide range of interest. When they visit a library, they don't check out books on only one topic, but rather sample many subjects. Linus Pauling said, "The best way to get a good idea is to get a lot of ideas."

What do you do with the information you acquire? Funnel

it through your mind and apply it to the central focus of your life. Remember, your ultimate objective is to sharpen specific skills in a particular area. In Proverbs 22 it states, "Do you see a man skilled in his work? He will serve before kings; he will not serve before obscure men."

When you have taken a realistic inventory of your life, begin to construct the strong foundation that will allow you to reach new altitudes.

6

Removing the Fear of Height

"Obstacles are those frightful things you see when you take your eyes off the goal."
— Hannah More

The president of a large chain of retail stores in Pennsylvania told me, "We have trained several potential managers who talked about success, worked toward achievement and came close to reaching the summit, but then something happened. Suddenly, for unexpected reasons, their life fell into disarray and we had to eventually drop them from our management program."

"How do you explain it?" I wanted to know.

"I believe that certain people are trapped in a cycle of self-sabotage" he stated.

Some extremely sharp individuals, time after time, come within sight of their goals, but never attain them. They are like the person who loses five pounds on a special diet, then gains it all back in one night of gluttony. Just as their best-laid plans are about to be realized they do something that brings chaos. Here are some examples.

- A college athlete received a huge bonus for signing with a professional sports team, but was cut from the squad for being unreliable — never showing up for practice on time.
- A woman who sold real estate was about to be named to a managerial position, when suddenly she stopped following through on paperwork and rarely returned her phone calls. Her fortunes reversed.
- An executive invested his life savings in a fast-food franchise and just as the unit was about to make a profit, he decided to take a three month vacation and the store folded because of lack of management,

Unfinished Adventures

For reasons that are difficult to explain, some people in sight of their objective will ruin their lives with drugs, excessive drinking, gambling losses, or sexual encounters that destroy their reputation and their marriage.

Why do people with promise become disappointments? There are many explanations.

Some individuals, because of the guilt of past actions, believe they do not *deserve* success. Or they may have been told "you'll never make it" so many times their subconscious believes it.

Others are actually frightened by the prospect of prosperity. They don't really want their lifestyle to change; they may have to give up their old friends if they begin to move in a higher economic circle.

Still others like the excitement of the hunt, but not the thrill of victory. As a result, their lives become a series of unfinished adventures.

You need to realize that the same determination which causes you to start your climb can allow you to finish. Push aside the nagging voice that tells you to turn back — whether it comes from outside or within.

"Many men fail because they quit too soon," stated Dr. E. C. Welch, founder of Welch's Grape Juice. "They lose faith when the signs are against them. They do not have the courage to hold on, to keep fighting in spite of that which seems insurmountable. If more of us would strike out and attempt the 'impossible,' we would very soon find the truth of that old saying that nothing is impossible . . . abolish fear and you can accomplish anything you wish."

The road ahead may be filled with a variety of twists and turns, but don't be afraid to press on. In the Old Testament there is an account of the twelve spies who investigated the land of Canaan. Only two had faith to believe the land could be captured. The other ten said, "We saw giants and we were in our own sight as grasshoppers."

When a man thinks he's a grasshopper, he acts like a grasshopper.

He sees himself much like that little insect; hopping around and never doing much that is constructive. Don't be afraid of the giants. Develop a strong belief that the same faith that brought you to the edge of the promised land will allow you to enter.

Rules for Mountain Climbing

The best way to remove the fear of height is to deliberately climb higher and higher. A true mountaintop experience will remove your apprehension and anxiety. Here are seven steps that will help your ascent.

Step 1: Attempt something extraordinary.

You can look in any direction and find people who have decided they'd rather be ordinary than to stretch and grow.

My friend John Mason wrote an inspiring book titled *An Enemy Called Average*. If you have not read it, get a copy. John says, "Mediocrity is a region bounded on the north by compromise, on the south by indecision, on the east by past thinking, and on the west by a lack of vision."

Our climb demands that we use our ingenuity to do something surprising.

We need to be like an inventor who has to depend on his or her imagination to make a living — deliberately shake up the creative juices by doing old things in new ways.

William Danforth said, "The best cure for a sluggish mind

is to disturb its routine."

Your actions need to exceed what is "normal" or expected. As Elbert Hubbard observed, "One machine can do the work of fifty ordinary men. No machine can do the work of one extraordinary man."

Step 2: Invest in yourself.

Reaching the crest of the summit is always the result of a tremendous investment of time, talent, and perseverance.

For example, Michelangelo's career as a sculptor and painter did not come easily. He worked for years to develop his abilities as an artist, but his renown was the result of giving of himself beyond the call of duty.

Michelangelo spent years lying flat on his back on a scaffold painting the fresco in the Sistine Chapel.

By the time he completed his historic masterpiece, he became almost blind from the paint that had dripped into his eyes. Because Michelangelo was willing to make a sacrifice, his art has been an inspiration to millions of people for more than four hundred years.

Step 3: View every action as valuable.

Your path to the peak is not accomplished in a few giant leaps, but is a series of hundreds of small steps. They are all equally significant.

An experienced mountain climber was asked to give his best advice to a group of novices. Here's what he told them: "When you are climbing up the face of a rock, you should always be assured of three good holds before moving up." And he added, "You have two feet and two hands to climb with. Three of these should be firmly anchored before making your next move."

That's good counsel. You will always move toward your goal with confidence when you take one secure step at a time.

Step 4: Move higher with humility, not arrogance.

Have you met people whose conceit and egotism seems to soar with each new advancement? Winston Churchill liked to say about such people, "There but for the grace of God, goes God."

Fortunately, life has a way of bursting our bubble of pride.

The popular actor, Tom Selleck, had an experience that taught him a lesson in humility. He recalls, "Whenever I get full of myself, I remember the nice, elderly couple who approached me with a camera on a street in Honolulu one day. When I struck a pose for them, the man said, "No, no. We want you to take a picture of us!"

Step 5. Climb with imagination.

When F. W. Woolworth opened his first store, a merchant nearby resented the competition and hung up a sign that read: "I have been doing business in this shop for fifty years."

The next day, Wooolworth made his own sign. On it were painted these words: "Established a week ago. All new merchandise."

You can guess who attracted the largest crowds.

There is always more than one route to the top. Don't be afraid to become adventurous.

I am reminded of the story of a credit manager who became worried when he studied a list of people with accounts past due. Even more, they were no longer active buyers.

The man decided on a unique approach. He sent all of them a bill for more than double the amount they owed!

As you guessed, the plan produced an amazing response. People who had paid no attention to the "correct" bills the store had been sending, were now highly upset. By phone and in person they demanded an explanation from the credit department. It worked. The department had a chance to apologize for the mistake — and at the same time work out arrangements for them to pay the "lower" amount they actually owed.

Step 6: Don't allow others to pull you down.

Do you know what happens when you break away from the pack? The pack gets angry.

When you climb a few steps higher than the competition, expect to feel their jealousy and resentment.

If given the chance, some would literally reach out and drag you back.

Have you ever seen a "dwarf" tree or shrub? The Japanese very cleverly stunt great forest trees and make them into potted plants by tying up the taproot. The trees live off the surface roots only.

The same thing can happen when you allow others to choke your dream. That is why you have to keep your attention focused on the crown rather than the crowd. When you finally are leading the parade, don't look back.

7. Allow yourself to be lifted by a higher power.

You are not climbing alone. The Creator has promised that He will guide you by His hand. The writer of Psalm 113 declared, "He raises the poor from the dust and lifts the needy from the ash heap."

Not only will you be uplifted, but you will have the stamina to continue your climb. In Isaiah 40 we read, "Those who hope in the Lord will renew their strength. They will soar on wings like eagles; they will run and not grow weary, they will walk and not be faint."

When we confront anxiety with faith and action, we no longer need to fear the height.

7

Here's the Plan!

"Every minute you spend in planning will save you at least three minutes in execution."
— Crawford Greenwald

Why do so many people drift through life with little sense of direction or accomplishment? Perhaps the answer can be found in the fact that only three percent of us have ever written goals for our life and less than one percent review their goals annually.

Most people spend more time planning their vacation than they do plotting the course of their future. In some cases they map out their trip day by day, even hour by hour and faithfully stick to their schedule. Can you imagine what would happen if they were as specific about the other fifty weeks of the year?

A goal has been defined as a dream with a deadline. It reduces the vision to something far more tangible. When you see your objectives in black and white they take on an entirely new meaning.

It is a misconception to believe that you need only one goal in life. Our interests and activities are much more complex.

We need specific, written objectives for each major area. For example:

- What goal do you have for your personal finances?
- Do you have a specific design for your social life?
- Have you written your objectives for your spiritual life?
- Do you have clear aims for your family?
- What goals do you have for your career?
- Have you detailed your objectives for your physical health?

One of the most important projects you'll ever undertake is to write a one year, five year and ten year plan for each domain of your life.

Don't trust your memory. Treat your goal-writing experience with the same importance as an agreement you would sign if you formed a business partnership. You are creating something even more vital — a contract with yourself.

Napoleon Hill said in his classic how-to-succeed book, *Think and Grow Rich:* "Anyone can wish for riches, and most people do, but only a few know that a definite plan plus a burning desire for wealth are the only means of accumulating wealth."

Whether you desire to create funds for your retirement or lose three inches of flab around your waist, principles of success are the same. Your mission must be so specific that it can be reduced to a written statement.

Time for an Exam

After you have written your goal, put it to the test. That is the only way you will know if it has a chance for success. Here are twelve measuring sticks for each of your written objectives.

1. Is my goal specific?

A vague wish such as "I want to be happy," or "I'd like to have more friends," will not make the grade. If your written goals are not precise you will never know when you reach your destination.

The object of your intent cannot be floating "out there" in some hazy future. It is not a mirage in the distance. You must be able to give it a name, a place, and a written description that leaves no uncertainty.

Be a rifle, not a shotgun. The cross-hairs of your telescope should be able to pinpoint your target.

2. Is my objective fixed and immovable?

An experienced outdoorsman can move from point A to point B in a forest because he has faith in his compass. He knows that it will always be pointing due north and he can calculate his current position with accuracy.

Oliver Wendell Homes stated, "The greatest thing in this world is not so much where we are, but in what direction we are moving." Who does the moving? *We* do.

When you write your goal, describe it in terms of being firmly anchored and secure.

3. Is my goal visible?

The athlete who sets an Olympic record in the high jump or the pole vault doesn't run toward the bar with his eyes closed. From the moment he begins the run to the crossbar his attention is totally focused on his goal.

The visibility of what you desire provides the necessary motivation to see it come to fruition.

4. Is my target challenging, yet attainable?

There is an art to goal setting. If your purpose requires little effort, you will be quickly bored and turn away from your plans. At the other extreme, if you choose an objective that is totally unreasonable, you will mentally resign before venturing the first step.

Look for a challenge that is beyond your grasp, but within your reach.

Start moving toward a prize you know you can accomplish with commitment and extra effort. When you are successful at hitting small objectives, you will be ready to expand your horizons and be challenged even more.

5. Is it ethical and honest?

What good is arriving at your destination if it leaves you feeling remorse or shame? It seems that every day we read the story of someone who has attained great success through fraud and deceit. A physician bills Medicare for surgeries that were not performed. A politician wins an election through vote fraud. A news reporter "fakes" evidence, attempting to make the story more dramatic.

If achievement requires deception, fraud, or even a little "white lie," the honors you may receive will be tainted. When given the choice, always take the high road.

6. Is my goal measurable?

Think about reaching your objective as attempting to make a touchdown in a game of football. Goals are measured in small steps. A football field is filled with lines and every yard is marked. Progress is usually measured by small gains. In fact you only have to move the ball ten yards to get a brand new start. When that happens you have a few more opportunities to move toward your goal.

What criteria will you use to measure your advancement? How will you gauge your progress?

7. Do all of my goals reinforce each other?

I have met individuals whose spiritual goals may be laudable, but when they compete in the arena of commerce, they play by an entirely different set of rules. As a result, their life is out of balance; there is no harmony, only discord.

Since you have clear objectives in several areas, be sure that all your wheels are turning in the same direction. If just one becomes locked, it can derail your best made plans.

8. Does my goal include a plan for its accomplishment?

Do you remember the answer to the question, "How do you

eat an elephant?" *One bite at a time.*

Dreams are only realized when they are broken down into manageable units of accomplishment. Here is how it works.

- It begins with the dream.
- The dream becomes a written goal.
- The goal becomes a detailed plan.
- The plan becomes a daily schedule.

What you accomplish in one day may seem small, but when your actions are related to a plan, every moment of your day becomes extremely productive.

When you have objectives in several areas, it isn't possible to give them each equal time. Periodically, you need to prioritize your goals so that your harvest will produce the best fruit.

9. Have I developed interim stairsteps to my destination?

For every item on your list, you should be able to write "Ten steps to reaching my goal." In some cases, you may have to detail even more hurdles to jump. Why is it important to create a game plan for reaching every goal?

When you have a check list, you will know where you are going. You can measure your progress and won't become lost and have to retrace your steps.

Remember, when you have ten "little goals" on the road to one victory you are constantly celebrating your success.

10. Do I review my written goals regularly?

Just as boards of every organization meet on an announced schedule, you need to set a specific time for meeting with yourself to examine, critique and reassess your progress.

Let me suggest that you have a quarterly review. Be honest about your successes and failures. You may even want to give yourself a "grade" on your performance and make a personal covenant regarding your aspirations for the next quarter.

11. Does my goal include a timetable for its completion?

Your written plan needs to be accompanied with an exact day for its fulfillment. Don't write, "I hope to reach my objective next fall." Be exact. Say, "I will complete this project on October 15."

Take your deadline seriously.

Remember, it takes the same number of hours to finish a task whether you do the work in a concentrated time-frame or stretch it out over many months or years.

12. Do I have faith that God will help me succeed?

Your Heavenly Father is not your enemy. He didn't place you on earth to fail, but to accomplish His vision for your life. Listen to these powerful words of Psalm 20: "May He give you the desire of your heart and make all your plans succeed."

It is good to know that when you create your plan, the great Creator is there to give you insight and inspiration. Let Him.

8

Who is Charting the Course?

"There is a time when we must firmly choose the course we will follow, or the relentless drift of events will make the decision."
— Herbert V. Prochnow

Children have very few choices. They are told when to rise, what to wear, how long they can play, what they will eat and what time they will go to bed. Parents are the absolute authority.

During the teen years things begin to change. Young people are given more freedom to choose, yet some have been sheltered so long they are unprepared for the decisions they are asked to make.

Finally, as young adults, they are told, "You're on your own!"

What really happens? Instead of becoming independent, self-assured people, millions allow someone else to make their decisions for them. They enter adulthood having very little experience handling personal responsibility.

In a desperate search for approval, they decide it is easier to conform than to blaze their own trail. Finally, they are enmeshed in a web of dependence on others.

I am certain you can name people you know who have fallen into that same pattern. They have not awakened to the fact they are no longer children. Instead of looking for protection, they need to become self-reliant.

Be certain your desires and aspirations are yours, and not those of someone else.

Solving the Puzzle

When a farmer purchases a piece of land, he knows exactly how many acres he owns, where the property lines are located, and what he plans to do to make the land productive. The deed is his. It's not registered in the name of his neighbor. He can look at his acreage and proudly say, "This land is my land!"

When you put a challenging jigsaw puzzle together, what is the first thing you usually do? If you are like most people, you pick out every piece with a straight edge and link together the parameters of the puzzle. You know where the borders are.

If your life seems broken into many pieces, start the restructuring process by establishing the boundaries. Determine exactly what belongs to you.

How do you link the missing parts together? It happens when you carefully concentrate your attention and energy on each piece. In the words of Winston Churchill, "It is a mistake to look too far ahead. Only one link in the chain of destiny can be handled at a time."

I've Decided!

Is what you are doing today the result of your own choosing? Did you make a personal decision or did you respond to the wishes of someone else?

Stop for a moment and realize that no one in the world except God and you can possibly know who you really are and what you truly desire.

Here is what behavioral researcher Shad Helmstetter states: "You are the only one who can ever determine whether you are successful or not. Taking that responsibility for yourself is an exceptional exercise in being responsible for you. The others in your life have their own successes to deal with — you have yours."

It is a life-changing moment when you rise and declare, "I've made a decision. This is what I plan to do with my future."

There is a tremendous confidence that becomes obvious when your direction is clear. As David Starr Jordan said, "The world stands aside to let anyone pass who knows where he is going."

Are you the architect of your own blueprint? Are you choosing the materials that will be used in the life you plan to build?

Coach John Wooden led UCLA to a never-equalled record of nine national basketball championships. The philosophy with which he coached his teams is this: "Failure to prepare is preparing to fail."

Two Creations

Earlier we discussed why having a clear vision of the future is vital. But is it truly *your* vision? Is what you see *your dream?*

Stephen Covey, author of *The Seven Habits of Highly Effective People,* believes we should always begin with the end in mind. He states, "All things are created twice. There's a mental or first creation, and a physical or second creation to all things."

The illustration Covey shares is what happens to the person who designs and constructs a home. He says, "You create it in every detail before you ever hammer the first nail into place."

What are the benefits of creating a masterpiece in your mind?

- First, it gives life to your plans.

- Second, it allows you the chance to revise your design.
- Third, it stamps your personality on the final product — it's yours!

You're in Charge!

Are you ready to enter uncharted waters? Will you venture into territory you have never seen?

John Glenn, one of the pioneers of outer space, states, "I suppose the one quality in an astronaut more powerful than any other is curiosity. They have to go some place nobody's ever been."

Before man reached orbit around the globe or took the first step on the moon, there were scientists who envisioned everything that would happen.

Listen politely to all the advice people have to offer. Read with great interest the counsel and wisdom of experts in your field. But when the time comes to fly, realize that you are the pilot. It is you alone who will make the decisions during both the takeoff and the landing.

Think about these words that were on a plaque in the lobby of a real estate office:

You can't control the length of your life,
But you can control its width and depth.
You can't control the contour of your countenance,
But you can control its expression.
You can't control another person's opportunities,
But you can seize upon you own and make the best of them.

9

The Miracle of Total Commitment

"Commitment unlocks the doors of imagination,
allows vision and gives us the 'right stuff'
to turn our dreams into reality."
— James Womack

When your heart is changed, everything changes.

It happened to me when I was twenty-three. On my way back from a journey to several countries in Africa and Europe, I made a brief stop in Cardiff, Wales, to visit a family my parents had known for several years.

The Brewster family had a sixteen-year-old daughter named Anne and I couldn't take my eyes off her.

"Would you like to take a walk down Cathedral Road?" Anne asked me that evening, trying to be polite to their guest from America.

We stopped for a cup of tea at a small restaurant downtown and I was more than fascinated by this lovely young lady. As I later joked to my friends, "She rolled her eyes at me, and I picked them up and rolled them back." I didn't know what hit me. I had searched the world for someone like this, and now she was here!

There was only one small problem. I was leaving for the States the next morning.

We walked back to her home on Dyfrig street and, as we reached the front step, I took her hand and announced, "I have something I want to tell you."

"What is it?" she asked, with an inquisitive smile.

"You are going to be my wife!" I whispered to her — almost shocked at my own words.

I wasn't too sure what to make of her reaction. Anne began to laugh.

Then she said, "You're serious, aren't you."

"Absolutely!" I responded.

As I began to pull her closer to me, the lights went on in the foyer. Her parents were waiting for us to come inside.

Everything was New

I don't think I had two hours of sleep that night. All I could think of was Anne. The next morning I told her again, "I meant what I said last night."

Anne rushed to her summer job and I took the train to London to catch a flight to New York.

As a result of that brief encounter, my entire life was never the same. My thoughts were distracted. My behavior was different. All I wanted to think about was that lovely young girl in Wales. On the plane I asked for some stationary and I wrote her the first of many, many letters. In fact, I wrote her almost every day. And I was overjoyed when her responses became more and more frequent.

It is difficult for love to blossom long-distance. I knew it would be personal contact that would really count.

I remembered the story of a fellow who fell in love with a girl from overseas and wrote her every day for a whole year. To show you how personal contact pays off, she married the postman!

Well, I was not going to let that happen to me. The next summer I was back in Cardiff. This time for a longer visit.

How did the story end? Four years from the time we met — when she was twenty and I was twenty-seven — we made our lifetime commitment to each other at a beautiful wedding in Wales.

When your heart feels the unmistakable tug of deep emotion, your world is forever changed. You don't need to look for the definition of the word "commitment," it is explained by experience.

The Power of the Future

Dr. Anthony Campolo, professor of sociology at Eastern College in Pennsylvania, believes that what you commit yourself to, will change what you are and make you into a completely different person. He says it is not the *past,* but the *future* that conditions you — "because what you commit yourself to determines what you are — more than anything that ever happened to you yesterday or the day before."

Here are the simple questions Campolo asks. "What are your commitments? Where are you going? What are you going to be?" He states, "You show me somebody who hasn't decided, and I'll show you somebody who has no identity, no personality, no direction."

There are two centers of influence that govern your actions. The *cognitive* domain is governed by your mind and the *affective* domain is controlled by your heart.

Which influence is the most powerful? I'm sure you already know the answer. The power of your emotions is infinitely stronger than your reasoning or logic. In the words of the German philosopher Nietzsche, "One ought to hold on to one's heart; for if one lets go, one soon loses control of the head too."

Character Traits

Since our feelings and passions are so dominant and commanding it is vital that our commitments are based on truth and strong values.

William Bennett, in his *Book of Virtues*, says, "The vast majority of Americans share a respect for certain fundamental traits of character: honesty, compassion, courage, and perseverance." These are virtues that should be the bedrock on which all change is based.

A person may be endowed with attractive physical characteristics, have a delightful personality and dress with style and flair. But such things are only the wrapping on the package. What is on the inside? What about the person's basic character?

Ray Kroc, founder of McDonald's, believes, "Money doesn't change men, it merely unmasks them. If a man is naturally selfish, or arrogant, or greedy, the money brings it out; that's all."

The words found in Proverbs 23 are as powerful now as the day they were written: "For as he thinks in his heart, so is he."

Those who build their life around the worship of intellectualism are missing the point. The thinking that matters most comes from your spirit and soul, not from your reasoning process or your mental prowess. In the words of Goethe, "All the knowledge I possess everyone can acquire, but my heart is all my own."

How Strong are your Convictions?

If I were to ask, "Tell me about your basic beliefs," how would you respond? Are there convictions at the core of your life that are unshakable?

It has been demonstrated throughout history that we are never truly certain how committed we are to anything until its truth or falsehood becomes a matter of life or death.

That is what the great English teacher and writer, C. S. Lewis concluded. He wrote, "It is easy to say you believe a rope to be strong as long as you are merely using it to tie a box. But suppose you had to hang by that rope over a precipice. Wouldn't you then discover how much you really trusted it?"

It is imperative that we develop a well-considered set of strong basic beliefs that will become a firm anchor in any storm — no matter how turbulent. John Stuart Mill put it this way:

"One person with a belief is equal to a force of ninety-nine who only have an interest."

We have been looking at the values that form the foundation of our character. When we have personal convictions that are secure, there is something else that happens. As a natural byproduct of inner belief is a confidence those around us cannot deny.

When skier Bill Johnson showed up at the Winter Olympics in Sarajevo, the news media had already labled him with the image of someone who was "cocky." Only a few weeks before the event, here is what he said to a reporter: "It's not a question of *whether* I win the gold, but what I do with it after I win it."

In Johnson's view, this was not bragging, it was *belief.* He was totally persuaded that those winter games belonged to him and that he was about to become a world champion. It came as a surprise to his critics, but he confirmed his confidence and became the first American man in history to win a Gold Medal in Alpine skiing.

What transformed Johnson from simply being an above-average skier to becoming the fastest in the world? It was total self-confidence and his commitment to win.

Johnson knew a great secret.

Here are the words an insurance executive printed on the back of his business card:

"One's destiny is not determined by what he possesses, but by what possesses him."

What are the things that have a lock on your heart?

Are You a Promise Keeper?

Your reputation is as good as your word. If you make a commitment, be prepared to live by it — regardless of the circumstances. King Solomon, heralded as one of the richest and wisest men who ever lived, declared, "A good name is rather to be chosen than great riches, and living favorably rather than silver and gold."

Bill McCartney, former coach of the University of Colorado Buffaloes, started "Promise Keepers." It is a renewal movement that involves hundreds of thousands of men worldwide. McCartney says, "If you were to take the word integrity and reduce it to its simplest terms, you'd conclude that a man of integrity is a promise keeper. He's a guy who, when he says something, can be trusted. When he gives you his word you can take it to the bank. His word is good."

How deep are the promises you have made to your family, your friends and to your work? What vows have you made to God, to your spouse, and to yourself? What about the future? Have you made commitments you will keep — no matter what?

10

Declare Your Intentions

"The mirror of the soul.
As a man speaks, so he is."
— Syrus

Have you ever had something in your character you wished would disappear? Perhaps it is uncontrolled anger, constant worry, or a pessimistic outlook.

There are two approaches to dealing with the problem. The first is to make a vow in secret and quietly work toward changing your behavior. The second is to make the decision and announce it to those who are close to you.

"But what if I fail?" you may ask. "Won't I be laughed at by my friends?"

Perhaps you are asking the wrong question. Why not ask, "What promises are easier to keep? Those I have made public or the ones I make to myself?"

I can guarantee you will find more motivation to succeed when you have made an open pronouncement.

Billy Graham was once asked why, at the close of his message, he asks people to get out of their seat and walk to the front of the platform for prayer. He responded, "There is something about making a public confession that seals it in your heart, confirms it to your friends, and makes it much easier to live the life you have openly proclaimed."

The same principle applies to announcements we make in other important areas. For example, you declare that you are going to be an optimistic, upbeat person at all times. After such a decree an interesting thing takes place.

When people expect you to be positive, you don't want to let them down. You live your intentions every day — every minute.

Finally, your resolution becomes your reputation. People say, "She is always so encouraging!" Or, "He never seems to have a bad day!"

The die is now cast. It becomes *easy* to live the life you have proclaimed since your decision is being bolstered by so many factors.

Shrinking Hurdles

Jim Harbin, a high school track coach in Cincinnati, says, "The event I love most is high-jumping. I like it because of the challenge it presents to students." He recalls, "When freshmen look at the height of the crossbar, they usually say, 'There's no way I could ever jump that high! And it's rare that someone clears the bar on their first attempt."

The coach says that his students become proficient because of two factors. He states: "First, you need to learn the right techniques; then you need to develop the will power it takes to lift your body over the bar."

Then a third thing occurs. After ability and belief, the student bolsters his faith with a firm affirmation and the hurdles begin to shrink.

Revealing your plans to the world can produce extraordinary results.

On a Mission

I have several volumes in my library by Wayne Dyer. When his first book came off the press, he took a leave of absence from his position as a college professor and was determined to make his book a bestseller — not relying on his publisher.

Dyer purchased several hundred copies of his book, *Your Erroneous Zones* and began criss-crossing the nation to tell people about the self-help volume. His confidence knew no bounds.

For the next six months, Dyer journeyed nearly thirty thousand miles to forty-seven states. Sales began to mushroom. During that time he personally sold and delivered more than fifteen thousand copies of his book to stores.

On his mission, he contacted feature writers and talk show hosts in every city that resulted in over eight hundred interviews.

What was the outcome of his self-proclamation? The book became a number one bestseller and Wayne Dyer's writing and speaking career was launched.

Would he have received the same response by keeping quiet? I seriously doubt it.

If you have a cause worth pursuing, proclaim it! The world won't respond to silence.

An Unusual Offer

Victor Kiam, the owner of the Remington Corporation, tells about the time a very determined young man came to him. He was seeking a job.

After Kiam finished reviewing his resume, he said, "You've got some talents, but there's really nothing available."

The young man would not take "No" for an answer. He continued, "I think there's a place for me here, even if it's not obvious yet."

Then he made an unusual offer to Kiam. "I'd like to work for thirty days without any compensation. If I don't fit in, I'll leave with no questions asked."

Kiam was so intrigued with the idea that he gave the fellow a chance. He was assigned to a department where the new employee soon discovered some problems and quickly outlined how he would solve them.

His talent was recognized and the young man was given full-time employment with Remington.

Two Declarations

When Glenn Cunningham was five years old, he suffered severe burns on his legs and the doctors told his parents he would spend the rest of his life confined to a wheelchair. They said, "He will never be able to walk again."

In a hospital bed, his skinny legs covered with scar tissue, Glenn made a vow. He announced, "Next week, I'm going to get out of bed. I'm going to walk." And that's exactly what he did.

His mother told how she used to look out of the window of their farm house and see Glenn holding on to an old plow, trying to make his twisted legs function. Before long he was not only walking, but running.

Then Glenn made a second declaration. He proclaimed, "Now I'm going to run faster than anyone has ever run." In 1934 he set the world's record in the mile and was honored as the outstanding athlete of the century at Madison Square Garden.

World-Changing Words

The biographies of men and women who have influenced history reveal the power of their spoken and written pronouncements.

- Moses announced he would lead the children of Israel to the promised land.
- Jesus declared "I am the way, the truth and the life."
- The Apostle Paul heralded the message of Christ to the nations of the world.
- Martin Luther launched the Great Reformation when he proclaimed, "The just shall live by faith."
- Thomas Jefferson shaped the future of America when he

wrote the Declaration of Independence.

- Winston Churchill inspired a nation when he said, "I have nothing to offer but blood, toil, tears and sweat."
- John Kennedy declared, "Ask not what your country can do for you, but what you can do for your country."

When you choose your course of action, believe it and declare it. Someone will be listening.

11

"I Just Can't Help It!"

"The chains of habit are generally too small to be felt until they are too strong to be broken.
— Samuel Johnson

A science professor who was studying the formation of habits made an amazing discovery.

He built a large glass tank and separated one third of it from the rest by installing a clear glass partition. Then he filled both sides with water. In the small side of the tank he placed a tiny minnow. In the larger area he placed a full-size bass. As the bass swam around and eyed the minnow, he dived for it but bumped his nose on the partition. For the next several days he lunged for the minnow but kept bumping his nose. He then did it only occasionally, until finally he stopped altogether. He had enough of hurting himself on that glass wall.

Next, the scientist removed the partition and allowed the minnow and the bass to swim around together. The bass stared at the tiny fish but never struck again.

Here was his big opportunity, but conditioning had changed his behavior.

All around us are people who mirror that fish. They have been hurt so many times their competitive edge is gone. They have lost their zest for living.

Habits take many forms. To some they are the seeking of pleasure; to others they are the avoidance of pain.

Daily Robots

We were all raised to learn certain routines. After practicing them dozens of times, we turn them over to "automatic pilot." Many become positive robots in our life that keep us healthy and safe.

Wouldn't it be sad if we had to be taught to tie our shoes again and again? But we don't. It is something we learn once and do it so often that now we don't even think about it.

Brushing our teeth becomes so automatic we sometimes forget we even did it. Our patterns of eating, thinking and dressing are so deeply imprinted in our subconscious that we pay them little attention. They are the necessary habits that take the worry out of daily life.

Unfortunately, there are two sides to the coin. Some routines become destructive forces and we are often powerless to break loose from their grasp. As St. Augustine said long ago, "Habit, if not resisted, soon becomes necessity."

I'm sure you have met people with behavior we write off

as habit: some constantly complain, others worry, or are sarcastic, or never show up on time. We say, "Oh, they are just human."

Family counselor H. Norman Wright believes, "Whatever you practice, you become. If you argue with people regularly, you become argumentative. If you criticize people often, you become a critical person. Repeated behaviors become habits."

In some instances, people don't *want* their conduct to change. They become smug and feel quite comfortable in their selfishness, laziness, bitterness or their lust.

Habits, however, can lead to conditions that are extremely serious. Countless people have developed either a physical or a psychological addiction to a behavior. It holds them in such a tight grip that their life is threatened. Here are just a few of the obsessions that cause people to be enslaved.

- Millions become physically and chemically dependent on alcohol and drugs.
- Some develop an obsession with cleanliness and the avoidance of contamination. They may wash their hands five or ten times every hour.
- Many become "control freaks" — they have a compulsion to dominate everyone around them.
- Food disorders including gluttony, anorexia (food avoidance) and bulimia (binging and purging) are life-threatening addictions.
- Many people are consumed by a preoccupation with entertainment — spending incredible amounts of time with computers, video games or a particular kind of music.
- People become hooked on exercise, diet, and physical conditioning and it controls every action of their life.
- "Mind games," or the pursuit of knowledge can become

an unquenchable thirst.

- Many lives are dominated by materialism — the craving to acquire and accumulate things.
- Money often becomes an addiction. It can take the form of uncontrollable spending, obsessive hoarding, or compulsive gambling.
- There are people who become so consumed with organizational detail and structure they lose sight of their original goal. They become caught in a web of perfection. Such people often have what is known as an obsessive-compulsive personality.
- The search for physical beauty can become addictive — including an obsession with cosmetics, suntanning, or clothing.
- People suffer from hypochondria — a constant fear they are afflicted with a physical illness, contrary to medical evidence.
- Religion, while a positive force for many, can become an addiction that leads to an unbalanced life, legalism or involvement with cults.
- Sex addiction (including pornography and eroticism) dominates the lives of countless people.
- The dangerous consequences of tobacco products is well documented.
- A "workaholic" is not someone who simply gives extra effort. It is a condition that is habitual.

We can become addicted to hundreds of behaviors — including the drive for success, the need to please people, volunteerism, and the dependance on unhealthy relationships.

"Compulsive behavior" is the term used for people who do things they know are harmful, but do them anyway.

Look again at the list of addictions above. Have any of

them touched your life? Have you been blindly lured to a behavior that you believe you can control, but in reality is governing you? Like a piece of cloth placed in a vat of dye, what we absorb, absorbs us.

If you have ever read the story of Jonah and the whale, you know one important principle: *You can run, but you can't hide.*

Be totally honest. If you are flirting with any potential addiction, back away quickly. They are silent killers that can invade your body, soul and spirit.

Analyze your behavior. Keep a personal diary for the next several days. Record every action — what you watch, what you eat and how you spend your time. Do any patterns concern you? Are there certain routines you may not have previously noticed? Are there activities to which you are strangely "pulled?"

The struggle with problems that seem beyond our control is not a recent phenomenon of contemporary society. Two thousand years ago the apostle Paul fought the same battle. In the seventh chapter of his letter to the church in Rome, Paul confesses, "I have the desire to do what is good, but I cannot carry it out . . . For in my inner being I delight in God's law, but I see another law at work in the members of my body, waging war, against the law of my mind and making me a prisoner of the law of sin at work within my members."

The Stages of Destruction

What is the compelling force that pushes or pulls us into a cycle of behavior we can't seem to conquer? What is the source of negative habits and addiction?

The psychologists with whom I have discussed this issue say that in most cases there is an "emotional emptiness" that creates a vacuum that cries out to be filled. Others have described it as a "love hunger."

Because of a desperate craving for attention, many people turn to behaviors they do not realize will eventually become devastating forces. They seek self-worth and find self-destruction.

Many debate whether a person's low self-esteem causes them to reach for a substitute, or whether turning to an addictive behavior causes low self-esteem.

Here is what is clear. All of our lives we are taught that when we have an ache there is a remedy. "If I just had the right pill, the pain will go away," they say.

Instead of calling the doctor for a prescription, many people look elsewhere for relief. They may purchase an expensive oil painting, give every waking moment to promoting a social cause, or buy dozens of romance novels as a means of escape. Unfortunately the fix is only temporary — and much too often these patterns are repeated again and again.

Then comes dependance.

What begins as an interest, becomes a pattern, and finally an addiction. Often, we do not recognize what is happening until it is too late.

Next, the individual comes face to face with the harmful consequences.

- They are rushed to the hospital with an overdose of drugs.
- There is a permanent police record for forgery or shoplifting.
- There is financial ruin that leads to destroyed credit and even bankruptcy.
- There is a serious medical problem from obesity or an eating disorder.

- There is an automobile accident caused by excessive drinking.

Finally, the person recognizes what has happened and is riddled with guilt and remorse. They are ashamed of their actions and, hopeful, reach the point where they realize they are in desperate need of help.

How do we become free of negative habits and destructive addictions? What do we do when we don't know what to do? That is the topic of our next chapter.

12

Break That Habit! Make That Habit!

"Motivation is what gets you started.
Habit is what keeps you going."
— Jim Ryun

We know the power of destructive habits and addictions, but what can we do to eliminate them? How can the iron gates be unlocked?

Several years ago I was in a seminar at the University of Miami graduate school studying methods to improve the skill deficiencies of young people. Our text was Robert Mager's book, *Analyzing Performance Problems*. I will never forget the subtitle printed on the front cover — "You Really Oughta Wanna."

The person who would rather loose their freedom than give up their cravings is not ready for true change. They first must enter the "wanna" stage.

- The heroin addict knows the drug will kill; he really oughta wanna quit.

- Mary oughta wanna lose that extra thirty pounds.
- Bill oughta wanna stop running up excessive bills on his credit cards.

Until there is desire, there will be no deliverance. We must develop the same hunger for change as the craving that addicts us.

Here are twelve steps to assist in banishing negative habits and replacing them with something positive.

1. Identify your habit.

Don't generalize about your problem. Call it by name and deal with it openly and honestly. You may want to spend considerable time working through your memories to identify the source and the history of the habit as it has affected your life.

Then examine its hold on you today. Can you recognize the "trigger" that sparks the unwanted behavior? Do you know the psychological patterns that bring you to a point of repeating the action?

2. Eliminate denial.

The person who believes they can halt the unwanted behavior any time they choose will usually deny there is a problem. When asked about their negative pattern, they say,

"What on earth are you talking about? I'm really fine."

Some people use a variety of defense mechanisms to deal with the issue. A close cousin of denial is repression — when we ban things from our conscious awareness. Others use suppression — avoiding the issue because the timing is not right. "I'll deal with that later!" they say.

To successfully address an addiction we must admit its existence and face it squarely.

3. Examine your motives.

Why have you chosen to change your behavior? Is it your heart-felt ambition or are you attempting to please someone else? Only you know the answer. Author Dwight Morrow says, "We judge ourselves by our motives and others by their actions."

Remember:

You will never give up what you believe is desirable. If your gut feelings don't tell you to eradicate the habit, it will never, never vanish.

4. Focus on what you want, not what you don't want.

Attempting to restrain an unwanted behavior seldom works because we concentrate so much attention on it. Diets, for example, almost always fail because those involved in the program are dwelling on only one thing — food. And what happens when we think about eating? We eat!

Dennis Waitley, in his book *The Psychology of Winning,* shares this insight: "One of the best guarded secrets is the kind of self motivation practiced by high achievers and effective leaders . . . it is imperative to concentrate our thoughts on the condition we want to achieve, rather than try to move away from what we fear or don't want." In other words, winners focus on the concepts of solutions rather than the concepts of problems.

Shift your attention to the solution, not the cause.

5. Use the principle of exchange.

People who attempt to give up cigarettes "cold turkey" usually return to nicotine within ten days. Why? By suddenly halting an addictive pattern they create an unsatisfied craving. Somerset Maugham was right when he said, "The unfortunate thing about this world is that good habits are so much easier to give up than bad ones."

Don't plan to ditch your habit; plan instead to exchange it. Carefully design your strategy. Decide what new activity you will add to your life to replace what you are leaving behind.

Substitution works. For example, you can deflect your urges by developing a taste for chewing gum instead of smoking.

What new habits should you choose? Elbert Hubbard offers this advice:

"Cultivate only the habits you are willing to be master of you."

6. Visualize your life with the negative behavior gone.

If you believe the extraction of your addiction will be like a dentist pulling your tooth without local anesthesia, you will avoid the experience at any cost.

Try to see is what your future is going to be like without the destructive habit at work. Can you picture yourself in better health, with fewer worries, and more friends? Hold that image and move toward it as the change begins.

7. Let the law of repetition work for you.

Just because you have instant coffee in your cupboard and a fast food restaurant down the street don't expect your old habit to immediately disappear when you snap your fingers.

The routines of your life didn't happen overnight. They are the result of constant repetition. I like what Mark Twain once said:

> ***"Habit is habit, and not to be flung out the window by any man, but to be coaxed downstairs a step at a time."***

Use the twenty-two day plan. Deliberately repeat a desired behavior for twenty-two straight days without fail. In almost every case you will find that the pattern becomes fixed — a permanent part of your life.

8. Use a multi-dimensional approach.

Those who supervise patients at clinics dealing with serious addiction will tell you that the problem will not be cured by simply depriving the patient of the addictive agent. The condition is complex and recovery requires a multi-faceted strategy.

Noted psychologists Frank Minirth and Paul Meier tell us that "To be truly healed of addiction, you must first find healing in the various dimensions of your personality, including your relationships, your feelings, your childhood memories, and your relationship with God."

9. Repair your broken relationships.

In far too many situations, habits drive a wedge between friends. A man in Ohio told his counselor, "When my cocaine habit reached $100 a day I used every trick in the book to find the funds to support it. I continually borrowed money from my friends under false pretenses. I took valuables from my parents' home to the pawn shop. I even broke off my engagement to the girl I was going to marry so that I could sell the diamond."

The young man recovered, but restoring the damage done to those he loved became a necessary part of the process. We cannot be totally healed until our relationships are reestablished.

10. Find an affirming support group.

Don't attempt to recover alone. You can receive tremendous support from those who have fought and won the same battle.

It is estimated that more than one million Americans are now actively involved in some 500,000 recovery groups. They range from The Twelve Steps of Alcoholics Anonymous to groups for compulsive shopping, codependency, compulsive overeating and sex addiction.

Why are positive friends important? We become more and more like those with whom we associate. In Proverbs 13 we read, "He who walks with the wise grows wise."

11. Set rational anticipations.

The person who declares, "I'm going to lose twenty pounds in the next ten days," is either setting themselves up for failure or they can expect to have some rather serious side effects in the next two weeks.

Make long-term lifestyle choices rather than chasing the latest self-help fads.

The woman who makes a permanent decision to eat foods that have a significant reduction of fat will find far greater success than one going on the "watermelon diet" — or whatever — for a week.

Remember, the weight accumulated slowly and should disappear the same way.

12. Ask God for total freedom.

People are often surprised that virtually all of the successful recovery programs have a strong spiritual dimension. They understand the place of faith and prayer in rebuilding our lives. In Psalm 18 we read, "It is God who arms me with strength and makes my way perfect."

Freedom is the result of knowing the source of truth. Jesus declared in John 8, "You will know the truth and the truth will set you free."

If there is a negative behavior you would like to put in the past, or a new habit you would like to establish, begin walking the path I have outlined.

Charles Reade gives this formula for sowing and reaping:

"Sow an act and you reap a habit.
Sow a habit and you reap a character.
Sow a character and you reap a destiny."

13

No More Excuses

"We have forty million reasons for failure, but not one single excuse."
— Rudyard Kipling

A farmer in Wyoming once asked his neighbor if he could borrow a rope.

"Sorry," the neighbor responded, "I'm using it to tie up my milk."

"You can't use a rope to tie up milk," responded the perplexed farmer.

"I know," said the neighbor, "but when you don't want to do something, one excuse is as good as another."

I am sure you have heard dozens of flimsy alibis people offer for avoiding action, not following through on their promises, or why they do not succeed. Often the logic defies explanation. If the individual doesn't know the true reason for their failure, they will invent one. Thomas Fuller was perceptive when he said, "Bad excuses are worse than none."

Others will rationalize — hiding the true motives of their beliefs and desires behind the veil of a plausible explanation.

Twenty Favorite Excuses

Many people don't wait for failure. They create reasons in advance that allow them to avoid even *trying*. Here are some of the favorite excuses people give for not embarking on the road to personal achievement.

1. I will probably fail, so why should I even try?

It would be ideal if we could all succeed on our first attempt. Unfortunately, that is not reality. For example, how many times did you fall before you learned to walk? Perhaps several hundred times. Repeated failure is not something to be scorned, it is a necessary ingredient for advancement.

What would happen if the research and development department of a pharmaceutical company feared failure? They would never endure the thousands of frustrating trials and errors it takes to bring one life-saving drug to the marketplace.

2. I already have too many problems.

The burdens most people bear are due to a *shortage* of success, not a surplus. Never make the mistake of refusing an opportunity because you think it will somehow add to your responsibilities.

Accept a new challenge as the chance to put your problems where they belong — in the past.

3. I like my life the way it is — why change?

Do you know what happens to a tree when it stops growing? It doesn't stay in a suspended state of development, it begins to die.

Never be satisfied with "business as usual." That is a dangerous route because complacency leads to collapse. Upsetting the apple cart could be a blessing in disguise.

4. People will criticize me.

The owner of a successful restaurant in South Carolina told me, "If I worried about what people said I would have quit this business long ago. My competitors are jealous, my old friends think I don't have enough time for them and my relatives are mad because I refuse to loan them any more money."

Don't be alarmed by your critics. Just be sure they are talking about you for being industrious rather than for being lazy.

5. I need more facts before I begin.

Did Christopher Columbus have all the information he needed before he set sail on his adventurous journey? Did Orville and Wilbur Wright know all the details of manned flight before their gasoline-powered aircraft soared through the air in 1903?

Dexter Yager, who built one of the world's largest Amway organizations, tells his associates, "When you have a dream, the facts don't count!"

6. I make too many mistakes.

Achievement and perfection are not synonymous. If your fear of making errors is keeping you from moving ahead, remember: It is virtually impossible to reach your destination without a trail of blunders.

The Swiss psychiatrist Carl Jung stated, "Mistakes are, after all, the foundation of truth, and if a man does not know what a thing is, it is at least an increase in knowledge if he knows what it is not."

7. Nobody wants to help me.

One of the great myths many people have about moving ahead is that "I have to do it by myself. Others have their own interest and don't really want to assist me."

That is faulty thinking. When people sense your sincerity and you ask for their help, they are usually honored to assist. Put God's great principle into action: "Ask and you will receive."

8. I'm not sure my goal is the right one.

After a speaking engagement in Minneapolis, I was signing some of my publications when a gentleman in his sixties told me, "I am looking forward to reading your book. I've had some good ideas but I have never been certain I had the right goal for my life." I told him it wasn't too late to decide.

I believe we know in our hearts what is right and wrong. If your objective is honest and does not cause harm to anyone, go for it!

What is the best goal? The one God has placed within you at that particular moment. Don't wait for conditions to become perfect or for an idea to totally overwhelm you. Start with what you have and allow it to grow.

9. I need more time to think about it.

Procrastination never pays — it *costs*. You can waste days, weeks, and even a lifetime thinking and wishing about possibilities. Without taking action you will someday sadly ponder what might have been.

You do not need more time, you need more toil.

10. I lack self-confidence.

If you have a shortage of self-assurance, join the crowd — so do the vast majority of those who try something new. Many executives who are masters of their own arena, become visibly shaken when seated in front of a television camera for an interview.

Don't be afraid to leave your comfort zone. Your confidence will grow with every new world you conquer.

11. It takes too long to succeed.

If you believe you need to reach your objective to find fulfillment, think again. When you know you are on the right path, every significant advance is a meaningful experience worth applauding.

The question is not the length of the journey, but the rewards along the way.

12. I don't have enough experience.

Launching a new venture has never required a prerequisite

of on-the-job training. The willingness to begin is all that is needed. British author Aldous Huxley says, "Experience is not what happens to a man. It is what a man does with what happens to him."

13. I would be embarassed if I failed.

The fact that you attempt something and are unsuccessful is no reason for humiliation or shame. It should be viewed as a badge of honor.

The real embarrassment comes when someone points out that you never really tried.

14. I have problems sticking to a schedule.

A man who recruits employees for a parcel delivery company told me about a young man who used as his excuse, "I don't think I'd be good at something that required such a detailed time schedule."

"What did you tell him?" I asked.

"Well, perhaps I was a little blunt, but I told him he probably already had a timetable — one that included dozens of things that were likely wasting his time."

People need to turn their schedule for failure into an agenda for achievement.

15. I'm not an enthusiastic person.

Determination is more important than zeal. Turtles are not enthusiastic, but they reach their destination.

Here is what is important: Your vision is the source of excitement.

When a creative idea is combined with a strong will, it will take more than a hurricane to hold you back.

16. I can't stay motivated.

There is no one alive who can stay inspired twenty-four hours a day. We all need time to back away from the action and recharge our tired batteries.

Instead of continually focusing on self-motivation, let your drive flow from your mission.

17. I don't feel I am creative enough.

There is not a rule that successful people have to be creative. Countless have become extremely successful by managing the talents of those who are enterprising and inventive. A Madison Avenue ad agency president said, "I'm surrounded by clever people. But I wouldn't trust one of them to keep the books or meet the weekly payroll."

We each have our own unique abilities that need to be developed to their zenith.

18. I don't have the right connections.

If you have a compelling idea, or an outstanding talent, you will not need to beg people to listen to your presentation. The word will spread and your gift will find its own reward.

A portrait artist told me, "The people who have helped my career the most are those who were drawn to my paintings at an obscure exhibit. I was not seeking them. They discovered me!"

19. I don't have the patience it takes to succeed.

Perhaps I will never understand those who are so anxious for their harvest that they pick green tomatoes and rock-hard peaches.

Remember: If you can't develop the stamina and endurance it takes to wait for success, you will have to develop the patience it takes to live with failure.

A train ride from Toronto to Vancouver does not become any shorter because of anxiety or impatience. Relax and enjoy the view.

20. I'm afraid to take a risk.

Ask yourself this question: "Do I believe in the future or do I fear it?"

A stock broker told me, "I meet people daily who have a great fear of investing in securities because they believe it is too risky — even though every historical chart shows a long-term upward curve."

The phrase "nothing ventured, nothing gained" applies to more than financial investments. Your ultimate achievement requires a step of faith.

Are you ready to eliminate your apologies and your rationalizations? Make a pact with yourself: *No more excuses.*

14

Get Tough On You!

"For a man to conquer himself is the first and noblest of all victories."
— Plato

The emperor of an ancient kingdom was walking along a road near his palace when he accidentally brushed against an old man whose steps were slow and uncertain. Immediately, the monarch stopped and apologized to the elderly gentleman. Out of curiosity, the emperor asked, "Who are you?"

The old man surprised him when he declared, "I am a king."

"A king?" the emperor asked. "Over what do you reign?"

Without hesitating, the old man answered: "I rule myself because I control myself."

He had conquered the most valuable kingdom of all.

We have each crossed the paths of people who attempt to take charge of everything — and everyone — in sight. They snap out orders like a military general or a dictator. But when it comes to controlling their own behavior, they suddenly become a coward. If there is the slightest pain or self-effort involved, they don't want any part of it.

I have met people who are tyrants in the office, task masters to members of their family and are even mean to their dogs and cats, yet when it comes to their own behavior, the opposite is true. Autocrats become pussycats when dealing with themselves. If it were possible they would sleep till the crack of noon and be pampered like a prince.

What change is necessary for success? Most people need a 180-degree turn in their conduct. They need to become tender with the world and tough on themselves.

The best management is self-management!

Take Charge of Your Time

An important measuring stick of how we govern ourselves is how we control the clock.

You say, "We can't regulate time. It moves at it's own pre-determined pace."

While the march of time is relentless and not subject to tampering, we can drastically change our actions so that we can accomplish much more with the moments we have available.

Here is what Fred Brooks, a systems designer at IBM, asked about the lack of time management goals. "How does a project get to be a year behind schedule?" He answered his own question: "One day at a time."

Instead of looking for major blocks of our day to capture, we need to start with something much smaller. Paul J. Meyer, founder of Success Motivation Institute, states, "Most time is wasted, not in hours, but in minutes. A bucket with a small hole in the bottom gets just as empty as a bucket that is deliberately kicked over."

Where do you begin to find extra minutes to expand your day? Here are a few ideas.

Dan Bouchard, a former professional hockey player said, "I would rather sleep only five hours and wake up at 5:00 or 5:30 and be in control of my time than to sleep later and spend the entire day controlled by time instead of controlling it."

Mary Kay Ash, founder of Mary Kay Cosmetics established what she called the "Five O'Clock Club." She knew that women had to cook breakfast, prepare lunches and get the kids off to school. To help her representatives be more successful she taught them the value of rising early, when it is quiet and there are no interruptions. That is when they could get their product orders written, plan their day and write "Thank you" notes.

It doesn't take much effort to create a significant amount of additional time.

Just setting the alarm thirty minutes earlier will give you an extra 180 hours a year. That is twenty-two additional eight hour days.

The Myth of Free Time

"What do you do with your free time?" someone asked after a leadership seminar I conducted.

"I don't have any," I responded with a smile. "To me, every minute is extremely valuable."

Oh, I know the person was talking about what I did when I wasn't working, but we discussed the fact that we need to place a much greater value on each minute.

If someone stole a piece of jewelry we would report it to the police. But what do we do about the thieves who constantly steal our precious moments?

How much are you paid each hour? That's how much someone is stealing when they dominate sixty minutes of your time.

B. Eugene Griessman, in his book, *Time Tactics of Very Successful People*, relates the story of the CEO of a large corporation who brought a "money clock" to the executive conference room. As each person walked into the room he said, "I'd like you to punch in. The time clock is over there."

Says Griessman, "The clock, which was programmed with the hourly cost of each attendee, calculated the amount of time that was elapsing and the total cost of the meeting in dollars." The CEO made his point clear. Meetings that last too long may seem to be free, but in reality are very costly.

Make the Minutes Count

The best way to take charge of your schedule is to create

a daily routine — and stick with it. Here is what was suggested by one time management consultant:

"Do time" — 8:00 a.m.to 10:00 a.m. This is when you complete your major projects of the day.
"Call time" — 10:00 a.m. to noon. Concentrate on both making and returning your phone calls.
"See time" — 1:00 p.m. to 3:00 p.m. Here is when you schedule personal interviews, either in or out of the office.
"Plan time" — 3:00 p.m. to 5:00 p.m. Set this period aside for becoming totally prepared to meet the objectives of tomorrow.

The great value in breaking your day into workable sections is that you can digest one major activity at a time, rather than dealing with what seems like scrambled eggs or a large bowl of spaghetti.

Here are some tips for personal organization.

- Use a checklist for accomplishing your daily objectives. As Will Rogers said, "Don't let yesterday use up too much of today."
- Make wise use of your commute time. Driving is not for daydreaming. Try listening to a self-help program or dictating letters you need to write.
- Take notes on the important things you hear. It's been said that a short pencil is better than a long memory.
- Don't let clutter cause you to be disorganized. Your desktop is not for storage. Turn your piles into files.
- Tackle the toughest job first. Start your day with the most time-intensive, difficult task on your schedule. Everything else will seem like a piece of cake.

- Learn the art of saying "No." Don't accept every task that is thrown your direction.
- Schedule shorter appointments. What happens if you plan interviews one hour apart? More than likely you will have one hour conversations. Try building an appointment calendar in fifteen minute blocks.
- Adopt a "Do It Now" philosophy. A Chinese proverb says, "The best time to plant a tree was twenty years ago. The second best time is now."

Perhaps we need to be like airline pilots and take a "checkride."

About every six months a commercial pilot in the United States is obligated to take a checkride. What is the purpose? That is how it can be determined if the pilot has begun to drift into bad habits. The flight doesn't determine whether or not the pilots are competent. That has already been established. The checkride makes sure they stay in absolute peak performance.

"Be careful, then, how you live," wrote the apostle Paul in the fifth chapter of his letter to the Ephesians, "— not as unwise but as wise, making the most of every opportunity."

Resolve to become a take-charge person — starting with you!

15

Skidmarks on the Road of Life

"It doesn't matter how much milk you spill as long as you don't lose your cow."
— East Texas saying

"Why don't we make some hand puppets? I asked my older sister, LuWayne.

"What for?" she replied. "I don't know anything about puppets."

"Well, I thought we could do a show for the kids in Sunday School tomorrow," I responded.

It was a hot Saturday afternoon in Granite City, Illinois, a small town across the river from St. Louis. My father, who was a minister, was conducting a series of meetings at a church and my sister and I were bored. I was twelve years old at the time.

We knew absolutely nothing about puppets but used our ingenuity. We made the heads by taking a wad of wet tissue paper and mixing it with some glue to form a round ball that would fit on our finger. When the two "heads" were dry, we painted on the eyes, nose and mouth. Next we found some pieces of scrap cloth and, with a stapler, made what looked like clothing for our two characters.

Locating a large cardboard box, we cut an opening in it and had a rough rehearsal for our show.

The next morning about thirty excited boys and girls sat on the floor in front of our makeshift stage and the puppets made their debut.

It was a disaster. Just as I got to the part where David was about to throw five smooth stones at the giant, the head fell completely off my puppet. In our panic, we forgot many of the things we had planned. Plus, my sister's voice certainly didn't sound like Goliath.

Somehow we made it though the program but decided we would probably never try to do a puppet show again.

Out of the Past

Several years later, when I was half way through a Master's degree program at Ohio State University, my telephone rang on a cold February morning.

"You don't remember me," stated the voice at the other end of the line, "but I was at the church your family visited in Granite, City, Illinois, about ten years ago. I remember that you and your sister did a puppet show for the children in the basement of the church."

"Well, you sure have a good memory," I responded. My mind was racing to try to remember an event I had long since forgotten.

"Do you still do puppets?" the man inquired.

"Why do you ask?" I wanted to know.

For the next five minutes he began to tell me of a rather large project he was in charge of in the organization where he now worked. "We are putting together a team that will travel to 27 countries on five continents this summer to present programs to young people. I thought a puppet show would be great because we could translate the scripts and tape record the programs in several languages. I think you and your sister would be a great addition to the team."

Then he asked again, "Do you still do puppets? Are you interested?"

"You can count on us," I told him, trying to hide my exhilaration. "We'll be ready."

I called my sister and said, "LuWayne, you are never going to believe this!" Then I told her the story of what was about to happen.

A few months later, as we were flying across the Atlantic on a four-motor Lockheed Constellation between Recife, Brazil, and Dakar, Senegal, the impact of how this exciting journey came about hit me with full force. I thought, "It's amazing what happens when you fail! We did the world's worst puppet show and it led to the trip of a lifetime!"

Never underestimate anything! What you consider to be a failure may open a door you never expected.

In the Game

All my life I have heard the phrase "Big doors swing on

small hinges," and now I know how true that saying is. Since that experience I have treated trivial matters with much more respect. They may lead to unexpected surprises.

Today, I continue to value my mistakes and can identify with the motivational speaker who said,

"Every time I stub my toe it reminds me that I wasn't sitting down. I was actively involved."

It is only when you are in the game that you have a chance for success. Wayne Gretzky, the famous hockey player, remembered the comment of one of his early coaches who was frustrated with his lack of scoring in an important game. The coach made his point when he told Gretzky, "You miss 100 percent of the shots you never take."

Your chances for steady growth are much greater when you keep things in perspective. You can eventually reach the point where *even when you lose, you win.*

Chris Evert Lloyd, the only woman to win the U.S. Open Tennis Championship six times, had her share of losses. Yet, even in defeat, she maintained a positive outlook.

Here's how she reviewed her professional career. Chris says, "Losses were always a relief. They took a great burden off me and made me feel more normal. If I won several tournaments in a row, I got so confident, I was in a cloud." Then she added, "A loss got me *eager* again."

Valuable Lessons

What happens when you attempt one of your unique ideas and fail? That is the time to admit your mistake and move on.

When the Coca-Cola Company introduced its "new" formula a few years ago, it took less than eighty days for them to bring back its original formula as "Coca-Cola Classic." Rather then further anger their loyal customers and lose more of their market share, they openly admitted their mistake.

Remember, you fail much more than you win. That is why you need to see every mistake as a valuable lesson. In the words of Ilka Chase,

> ***"The only people who never fail are those who never try."***

The apostle Paul saw hope in the midst of problems. He wrote in his second letter to the Corinthians, chapter 4, "We are hard pressed on every side, but not crushed; perplexed, but not in despair; persecuted, but not abandoned; struck down, but not destroyed."

No Bed of Roses

Baseball's home run king, Hank Aaron, said, "I have always felt that although someone may defeat me, and I strike out in a ball game, the pitcher on that particular day was the best player. But I know when I see him again, I'm going to be ready for his curve ball. Failure is a part of success. There's no such thing as a bed of roses all your life. Failure will never stand in the way of success if you learn from it."

As humans, we are all prone to errors. We're not like the paratrooper who was in training at the military base in Ft. Benning, Georgia. He asked his top sergeant, "Sarge, how many jumps do I have to complete to graduate?"

"All of them." replied the top sergeant.

Fortunately, most of us are not involved in an endeavor where mistakes are fatal. A paratrooper can't afford to make an error. We can. And they give us a real-life education.

Don't Worry, Dad!

When our son, Ian, was in the eighth grade he had his first serious girlfriend. For about one week he could hardly stop talking about her. Then, suddenly, we didn't hear another word about the young lady.

"What happened to your girlfriend?" I asked. "You haven't been talking about her in the last couple of days."

"Oh, didn't I tell you?" Ian said, rather unconcerned. "We broke up." Then he added, "Don't worry dad, she's just a skidmark on the road of life!"

After a silent chuckle, I advised, "Don't wear out too many sets of tires!"

A Better Idea

The next time you are worried about your failures and mistakes, read these words. They were printed on the back of a church bulletin by an anonymous writer:

Lord, are you trying to tell me something?
For failure does not mean I'm a failure;
It does mean I have not yet succeeded.

Failure does not mean I have accomplished nothing;
It does mean that I have learned something.
Failure does not mean I've been disgraced;
It does mean I dared to try.
Failure does not mean I don't have it;
It does mean I have to do something in a different way.
Failure does not mean that I have wasted my life;
It does mean that I have a reason to start over.
Failure does not mean that I should give up;
It does mean that I must try harder.
Failure does not mean that I will never make it;
It does mean that I need more patience.
Failure does not mean you have abandoned me;
It does mean you must have another idea.

16

How to Measure Your Progress

"The rung of a ladder was never meant to rest upon, but only to hold a man's foot long enough to put the other somewhat higher."
— Thomas Henry Huxley

On one of my journeys to East Africa I was invited to go hunting with some businessmen who lived in Tanzania. We traveled in a four-wheel drive vehicle toward the base of Mount Kilimanjaro.

I must admit I have never been much of a hunter and the experience was new to me. They handed me a Winchester 300 rifle and we began walking near the edge of a forest. There was a vast plain just ahead.

It was not long until we saw a herd of gazelle running with some other animals across the open field. "Don't shoot the hartebeest or zebra," I was told. They were off limits.

We were, however, allowed to hunt for gazelle — one of the swiftest animals in the world. They are in the antelope family and have u-shape black horns with ring-like ridges.

In my scope I saw one animal of the herd and I pulled the trigger. Wham! I thought the kickback had permanently injured my right shoulder. I also missed the target. "Am I too slow or are they too fast?" I asked.

"Let's get a little closer," the guide whispered.

For about ten minutes we quietly made our way closer to the area where the gazelle were feeding on the grasses. This time, when I looked through the scope attached to the rifle, the target was much, much larger.

I shot again and bagged a magnificent trophy. Our group took home several gazelle — enough to feed the children at a nearby school for more than three weeks.

That day I learned a valuable lesson:

If you want to enlarge the bull's eye, move closer to your objective.

Don't wait for the goal to come toward you — keep moving in its direction.

Start Measuring

On your journey of a lifetime it is important to keep track of your advancement. Let's examine eight ways to measure your progress.

1. Be fully aware of your starting point.

I remember attending a high school track meet when a star athlete was disqualified from the 100-yard dash because his toe was over the starting line. The young man was so intent on his goal that he totally ignored his take-off. He was heartbroken.

The first part of the word self-direction is *self.* Have you examined what you need to know about *you?* Even the smallest piece of information is worth discovering.

In the words of an old English proverb, "A good beginning makes a good ending."

2. Set your own timetable.

When the Baltimore baseball star Cal Ripken shattered Lou Gehrig's once-immortal record of 2,130 consecutive games, Ripkin was humbled by the accolades. Said a modest Ripken, "The game challenges you to do your very best, day in and day out. That's all I've ever tried to do."

The goal Cal set for himself was not to break Gerhig's record, but to be the most consistent player posssible. As a result the heralded shortstop played for more than thirteen seasons without missing a game.

A wise man once said, "Be not afraid of going slowly; be only afraid of standing still."

3. Have some predetermined check points.

On my car is an on-board computer that tells me more information than I need to know. I must admit, however, when I am on a long trip I enjoy punching in the number of miles to my destination and watching the computer go to work. Based on my current speed it constantly calculates the estimated time of my destination.

Are you aware of your progress? Just as a yardstick is broken down into feet and inches, you need to establish check points on your journey.

4. Do not compare your progress with others.

Perhaps the greatest mistake people make in moving toward a goal is to compare their advancement to those on their right or left.

For many years our educational system has measured the academic potential of college-bound students on the SAT scores they attain. While students were compared with each other, the overall scores for the entire group continued to decrease.

What is the value of outscoring someone else and not making the advancement you need? You are not in competition with the world, you are only in a contest with *you*.

5. Use "zero based" measuring.

There is only one valid way to assess your headway — and you can do it yourself. Your progress must be viewed in personal terms.

Don't ask, "How do I compare with someone else. Ask, "How far have I come from where I began?"

The true starting point is *your* place of departure. Any other measurement or comparison will give you a false reading. Your key to success is personal growth. I believe it will be an eye-opener when you see the actual progress you are making.

6. For every step back, take two steps forward.

Perhaps you have felt like a friend of mine who recently confided, "I feel like I'm rowing upstream. I paddle as fast as I can to get ahead, then something will happen and I drift back downstream."

The moment you feel yourself sliding, that is the time to go on the offensive. For every move back, take at least two — even three — great leaps forward.

Do everything in your power to achieve the "ratchet" effect." That is a mechanical device where a hinged catch engages a toothed wheel in such a way that it prohibits backward movement. Put the brakes on your reverses and then push your accelerator to the floor.

Keep moving forward.

7. List the "side benefits."

Goals are great, but don't overlook the "extras" you receive along the way.

For example, if you decide to take a walk up a mountain path to see the autumn leaves, you will receive more than you anticipate. Your mind is stimulated by the colorful display. Your body feels better because of the physical exercise. And your soul is refreshed by the beauty of God's creation.

8. See the finish line as a new starting point.

Millions of people have had such a fixation with the day of their retirement that they mentally — and often physically — die not long after that long awaited event. They saw retirement as the end, not as a fresh start.

People like to say, "It's not over till it's over." But that is not true because it's *never* over. There is an eternity ahead.

Happiness is not something to achieve, it is something to do. Your objective should never be seen as a final destination, but as a launching pad for an even greater challenge. In the words of Robert Schuller, "Every end is a new beginning."

17

It Takes Two!

"Coming together is a beginning;
keeping together is progress;
working together is success."
— Henry Ford

Driving through the state of Illinois on my way to a speaking engagement my eyelids began to droop. It was not the first time I had felt sleepy at the wheel, so I had a few tricks to keep myself awake. I've tried turning up the radio full blast, screaming at the top of my lungs, sticking my head out of the window to get a cold blast of air, chewing gum, even driving with my shoes off.

Once, when my wife was with me I slapped my face rather hard. Surprised, she asked, "What in the world was that all about?"

"I felt a little sleepy," I responded.

A few minutes later, as we were driving, all of a sudden my wife turned and slapped with more than a little force. "What was that for?" I asked, rather shocked.

She smiled and said, "You looked a little tired, dear."

Well, on this particular trip I was by myself and I stopped

at a roadside service station that had a food mart. I thought, "Perhaps if I eat something hot and spicy it will keep me going."

On that day in early June I bought a package of barbecued Corn Nuts — those large kernels of corn that look like they have exploded.

When I returned to my car and continued my journey, I opened the packet and noticed there was a small clear plastic envelope inside. In it I could see six large kernels of corn with a note attached: "If you plant these seeds you will have the largest corn known to mankind — the same type used to produce Corn Nuts."

I couldn't wait to get home. We were living in the state of Missouri at the time and I was anxious to plant the seeds in my little garden.

Time for Planting

"Anne, look what I have," I said as I walked into the kitchen. Showing her the small packet of seeds, I announced, "We're going to have the biggest corn in the world!"

"Please, not in this neighborhood," she protested. "Don't embarrass me!"

Well, I partially followed her wishes. I took one of those seeds and carefully planted it in the far corner of our lot. Every day I made sure it had some water and I watched with anticipation as it sprouted through the earth. By late August that one stalk was taller than me and there were two ears of corn on it. When I thought it was time for my big harvest, I pulled off the two ears and brought them into the house.

"Look, dear, we've got giant corn!" I said with great pride.

But when I "un-shucked" my two prized ears of corn, I

was in for a shock. There were only three or four large kernels of corn on each one, surrounded by hundreds of tiny, undeveloped kernels.

Disappointed, I took the two rather ugly specimens to my neighbor who used to be a farmer. "Let me see the rest of it," he asked.

"The *rest* of it?" I responded. "That's all there is. I only planted one seed." He chuckled and gave me a lecture on the genetics of corn. He explained, "The wind blows the pollen out of the tassels of one ear and it is caught by the sticky threads of silk on another ear. It's like cross pollinating apple trees." He concluded by saying, "To have beautiful corn you have to plant *lots* of it. Otherwise it will be useless."

It was a lesson I will never forget.

Later, as I thought about my single stalk of corn I realized that people are the same. We were not made to grow alone.

When we fail to link our lives with others we become unpleasant. In some cases we self-destruct.

The $6,000 Eggs

I laughed when I heard what happened at a banquet where they were celebrating the 25th anniversary of the pastor of a church. After many tributes were given, the minister's wife walked to the podium and handed her husband a basket. In it were two eggs and a check for $6,000.

"What are the eggs for?" the curious husband wanted to know.

"Well, every time you preached a bad sermon, I put two eggs in the basket."

"And what about the $6,000?" he asked.

"Oh, every time I got a dozen eggs I sold them!"

They were quite a team!

Flying in Formation

The advantages of a united effort are quite amazing.

Have you ever seen a flock of geese flying in their traditional "V" formation? Engineers have learned that each bird, by flapping its wings, creates an uplift for the one that follows.

Together, a flock of birds gains as much as seventy percent greater flying range than one bird could accomplish alone.

It is the same in any group of people, large or small. When we combine our talents and creativity we are far more productive than when we each go our separate ways.

In virtually every area of human endeavor, teamwork is better than going solo.

- God didn't create only one person in the garden, He

made *two*.

- It takes more than one wing for a bird to soar and fly.
- The president of the Ford Motor Company can't produce cars by himself. It takes a united effort.
- The greatest football quarterback of all time would be helpless without a strong offensive line.
- The Constitution of the United States begins with the words: "We the people."

The writer of Ecclesiastes declares:

"Two are better than one, because they have a good return for their work: If one falls down, his friend can help him up."

He Found Help

When we read the inspiring books of Norman Vincent Peale, it is hard to believe that as a young man he was extremely shy and had low self-esteem. Once, in a college economics class, he shuffled into the room and found a seat on the back row — hoping he wouldn't be noticed.

To his deep distress, the professor called on him to explain a point in the day's lesson. Norman was a good student academically, but terrified of speaking in public.

When he stood to his feet, his knees were knocking and his

body was nervously rocking from one side to the other. His attempt to give a coherent answer was a disaster and he slumped back in his seat.

At the end of the period, the professor said, "Peale, please remain after class. I want to talk with you."

Norman was quaking in his boots. When the students left, the professor said, "I'd like for you to come up to the front and sit across from my desk."

After an awkward silence, the teacher asked, "What in the world is wrong with you, Peale? You are doing good work in this class and you will probably get an 'A.' But when I ask you to speak, you appear horribly embarrassed, mumble sort of incoherently, and then slump red-faced into your seat. What's the matter with you, son?"

Looking at the floor, Peale replied, "I don't know, sir. I guess I've got an inferiority complex."

The professor asked, "Do you want to get over it and act like a man?"

Peale nodded and quietly replied, "I'd give anything to get over being the way I am, but I don't know how."

The professor's face softened as he continued, "You *can* Norman, by doing what I did to get over my inferiority feelings."

Peale looked up and exclaimed, "You were the same way I am?"

"Yes. That's why I noticed the similar traits in you," the professor said.

"What did you do about it," Peale wanted to know.

He received a simple, but profound answer. The teacher said, "I just asked God to help me. I believed that He would and He did."

From that moment forward, Peale took the professor's advice and it worked. You can call it psychology, faith, seed planting or whatever you want, but by forming a team with the Lord, Peale eliminated his shyness in record time.

When you are not certain where to turn for help, God is always there. He not only created a world based on unity and accord, but is ready to demonstrate it every day.

18

Ten Rules for Team Players

"The people with whom you share your goals will play a major part in whether or not you reach the goals."
— Zig Ziglar

In the last chapter we learned something from birds. But there is also something we can be taught from the bees.

My friend Charles Dygert in his book, *Success is a Team Effort,* tells the fascinating story of how bees survive the bitter cold of winter through a system of cooperation.

Says Dygert, "Bees live through cold temperatures by a strategy of committing to a common cause through mutual aid. They form into a ball and keep up what amounts to a non-stop motion that resembles a dance."

The process is totally unique. "To accomplish their goal," says Dygert, "the bees change places; those that have been on the cold outer edge move to the center, and those at the center move out. If those in the middle insisted on staying there —

keeping the others at the edges — they would all perish."

Playing by the Rules

The survival of nations, businesses, families and individuals depends on how we apply the strategies of working together.

Can you imagine what life would be like if there were no laws, no boundaries and no accepted standards of conduct. There would be utter chaos.

Would our favorite sports continue without regulations? I doubt it. That is what puts the fun in the game.

If you plan to be a team player, here are ten rules to follow.

1. Develop a team vocabulary.

You can know almost in an instant whether someone is a team member or is playing by their own rules. It is as simple as listening to their words.

Recently I attended a conference that had as its theme, "Cooperation in the Workplace." It became clear that some speakers were communicating the message in a manner far superior than others. What was the difference?

The executives who had an "I" vocabulary were missing the mark. Those who constantly used "we," not only held the attention of the audience, but in my informal survey were much better received as personalities.

2. Spend time with successful people.

Winning not only takes skill, it takes a special attitude. One of the best ways to develop a successful mind is to surround yourself with positive people.

Napoleon Hill recommended the practice in his book, *Think*

and Grow Rich. Discussing the Master Mind principle, he wrote, "When a group of individual brains are coordinated and function in harmony, the increased energy created through that alliance becomes available to every individual brain in the group."

An investment banker told a group of college business majors,

"If you want to make $100,000 a year instead of $50,000, start hanging around people who make $100,000."

3. Ask people to join your cause.

Don't hesitate to recruit people to the idea you believe in. Friendships that are formed around a mutual interest have a better chance to blossom and grow.

In my travels as a speaker, I see first hand how people become bonded to business associations, church organizations, alumni and special interest groups.

I have stood in the lobby of a headquarters hotel and watched arriving guests literally scream with delight as they spot their friends. It is the cause that brought them together.

4. Be genuinely interested in others.

Those who shower attention on people for business purposes or personal gain are soon exposed for their misguided motives. Friendships that last are based on both parties having the heart of a servant.

It has been said that life is much like the game of tennis — those who don't serve will end up losing.

Paul wrote in the second chapter of Philippians, "Each of you should look not only to your own interest, but also to the interest of others."

5. Listen closely to what people are saying.

Open lines of communication are the key to building strong alliances. Make it your objective to listen more than you talk, to concentrate on the real message being given, and respond by giving others your full attention.

"It takes two to speak the truth, wrote Henry David Thoreau, "— one to speak and another to hear."

6. Allow others to contribute their best talent.

Billy Martin, the famous New York Yankee, said, "No one can play whatever position they choose. If that happened in baseball, there'd be nine pitchers."

Great associations result from the blending of gifts. When people give their energy for the good of the team rather than for personal glory, the results can be spectacular.

7. Win through cooperation, not competition.

Sales and marketing executives have come to this conclusion:

You cannot compete externally if you compete internally.

What happens when ten employees are attempting to win the same prize? You have one winner, nine losers, and a great potential for bitterness and strife.

Continuing studies suggest that only fifteen to twenty percent of the population function well in an environment where they are to be competitive with others.

A much better attitude was expressed by Ron Hundley, who said, "My biggest thrill came the night Elgin Baylor and I combined for 73 points in Madison Square Garden. Elgin had 71 of them."

8. Balance criticism with encouragement.

The principles of team building are the same whether you are trying to manage the division of a company, coach a soccer squad or raise a family. You have to balance censure with praise, and correction with compliments.

Since most people are wounded by criticism, pour on much more sugar than salt.

9. Practice fairness.

There are two sides to every story — and sometimes more. To be a team player you often have to wear the hat of an arbitrator, a judge, a negotiator and a fence mender.

The question you must continually ask is this: Is it fair to all concerned? As writer Charles Brower said, "You cannot sink someone else's end of the boat and still keep your own afloat."

10. Learn to forgive.

There is no room for envy, resentment or hate on the playing field of life. Teams that win are comprised of individuals who know how to end grudges and patch up personal differences. They not only pardon, but they do it quickly and permanently.

Thomas Fuller wrote, "He who cannot forgive breaks the bridge over which he himself must pass."

When you play by the rules, you always win — regardless of the score.

19

The Prize-Wining Ingredient

"The people who get on in this world are the people who get up and look for circumstances they want, and, if they can't find them, make them."
— George Bernard Shaw

The great writer of fables, Aesop, told the story of a wagon master who was driving his team along a muddy lane with a full load, when the wheels of his wagon sank so deep in the mire that no effort of his horses could move them.

As the driver stood there, looking helplessly on, he began calling loudly upon Hercules for assistance. Before long the god himself appeared and said to him, "Put your shoulder to the wheel, man, and goad on your horses, and then you may call on Hercules to assist you. If you won't lift a finger to help yourself, you can't expect Hercules or anyone else to come to your aid."

The moral of the story is that heaven helps those who help themselves.

Somebody's Working

As we rush through our day, there is much we take for granted.

- We rise in the morning and casually read a newspaper that was compiled by hundreds of journalists — many of whom burned the midnight oil.
- We eat a slice of bread and never consider that a Kansas farmer spent hundreds of hours plowing fields, planting seeds, and harvesting the wheat that produced it.
- We drive in an automobile that is a collection of thousands of parts produced by tireless workers in factories around the globe.
- We make a phone call that travels through wires that countless workers have constructed and maintained.

It is estimated that the items we use every day — from the clothing we wear to the roads we drive on — are the result of the labor of over a million people. What has produced our civilization? It's a four letter word called *work*.

As I was preparing this book, someone looked at the title and asked, "When I find out what I'm supposed to do, what happens next?"

"That's easy," I replied. "Start doing some serious work."

Nothing happens by accident. God created us with two strong arms for a reason. There is work to be done and we must do it.

Benjamin Franklin said, "All mankind is divided into three classes: those that are immovable, those that are movable, and those that move."

The vision you have for your life will drift by like a cloud if you don't fashion it into something tangible through your personal labor.

What is the prize winning ingredient of success? It is the willingness to do whatever it takes, for as long as it takes, until the goal is realized. And that may mean longer hours than you have ever worked.

Kemmons Wilson, the founder of Holiday Inns, built a vast network of hotels, yet never completed his high school diploma. It came as quite a surprise when, after his empire was established, he was invited back to the school he attended to give the commencement address to the graduating class.

Wilson began his speech by saying, "I really don't know why I'm here. I never got a degree, and I've only worked half days my entire life. My advice to you is to do the same. Work half days every day. It doesn't matter which half you work — the first twelve hours or the second twelve hours."

He wasn't joking. The person who is focused on a clear objective won't quit when the clock gives the signal. He or she is governed by mission, not by minutes. And there is an enormous difference.

It is sad that people around the world are devoting longer hours to labor, but out of financial necessity, not because of a desire for achievement that burns within them.

Can you imagine the productivity levels if people were self-motivated to accomplish their present tasks with zeal and passion?

Removing the Risk

The term "hard work" means different things to different people.

When you watch a television program that features a remarkable performance by a world champion gymnast, it is easy to overlook how much time and effort goes into one small motion.

Do you remember Nadia Comaneci? She was the five time Olympic gold medalist who won the hearts of people everywhere. Says Nadia, "If I work on a certain move constantly, then finally, it doesn't seem risky to me. The idea is that the move stays dangerous and it looks dangerous to my foes, but it is not to me. Hard work has made it easy."

Her practice habits reflect the thoughts of George Bernard Shaw, who said:,

"When I was a young man, I observed that nine out of ten things I did were failures, I didn't want to be a failure, so I did ten times more work."

What do employers look for and can't seem to find? They cannot locate people with the built-in self-starting quality called initiative.

Most workers respond to motivation, but they possess very little. They accept direction, but they demonstrate it sparsely. Instead, they are part of the passive work force whose physical body may be on the job, but their heart is far, far away.

Humorist Robert Benchly commented, "Anyone can do any amount of work, provided it isn't the work he is *supposed* to be doing at that moment."

It is time to move the gear shift from "Park" to "Drive." As author John Mason says, "Being on the offensive and taking the initiative is a master key which opens the door to opportunity in your life." He warns: "Don't ever start your day in neutral.

Every morning when your feet hit the floor, you should be thinking on the offensive, reacting like an invader — taking control of your day and your life."

Does success come before work? Only in the dictionary. In real life, labor is the pump that brings productivity.

The philosophy of Art Linkletter summarizes what it takes to turn better into best and average into achievement:

Do a little more than you are paid to;
Give a little more than you have to;
Try a little harder than you want to;
Aim a little higher than you think possible;
And give a lot of thanks to God for health, family, and friends."

When the signs of success begin to appear, build on your accomplishments. Instead of living week to week, try living peak to peak.

The marketing director for a vacuum cleaner company always asked this question at a meeting of his salesmen: "When is the best time to make a sale?"

His associates knew the answer. "The best time to make a sale is when you have just made one."

The first success builds up an enthusiasm that helps make the second sale.

We need to be like Hesekiah, the king of Judah who was written about in 2 Chronicles 31. The Bible records, "And in every work that he began . . . he did it with all his heart, and prospered."

The Achievers

Who are the people who deserve to be recognized as achievers? President Theodore Roosevelt described them forcefully when he wrote:

It's not the critic who counts;
not the man who points out how the
strong man stumbled, or where the doer
of deeds could have done better.
The credit belongs to the man who is

actually in the arena, whose face is marred by dust and sweat and blood; who strives valiantly; who errs and comes short again and again, who knows the great enthusiasms, the great devotions, and spends himself in a worthy cause; who at best knows the triumph of high achievement; and who, at worst, if he fails, at least fails while daring greatly, so that his place shall never be with those cold and timid souls who know neither victory nor defeat."

20

Do What You Love! Love What You Do!

*"It is not doing the thing we like
to do, but liking the thing we have
to do, that makes life blessed."*
— Johann von Goethe

Research tells us that nearly eighty percent of all workers dislike what they do for a living.

A woman in Colorado told me, "My husband and I both work two jobs, but our heart is not in our work. We are just marking time, trying to pay the bills."

The problem most people face is that they have been caught up in doing a job that is the inspiration of someone else — not them. Someone else had a vision to build a billion dollar bank, and they are working in it. Someone else felt a calling to establish a social agency and they are helping to carry out that call.

Knocking on Doors

Marsha Sinetar, an organizational psychologist, when talking about her past experiences, said, "The work I disliked the most was work I wasn't suited for. Once, for example I sold vacuum cleaners door to door. Now there's nothing wrong with that job, except I was painfully shy and basically introverted, and knocking on doors in strange neighborhoods was, for me, an unnatural act."

Says Marsha, "I was working my way through college and in desperate need of money, so I silenced my fears and told myself I could do it. The money was good, and that somehow made it all right. The only catch was my heart wasn't in it. I lasted one day."

How would you respond if someone conducting confidential research asked you these questions:

Does your current employment give you the chance to express your greatest talent?

If you could receive the same amount of money in a totally different occupation, would you make the change?

Which of the following best expresses the reason you are staying with your present job?

A. I need the money.
B. I'd lose my personal benefits if I quit.
C. I enjoy being around my fellow workers.
D. I feel obligated to my boss.
E. The company needs me.
F. It gives me a chance to express myself.
G. It is truly what I love to do.

What message do your answers reveal? On a scale of one to ten, how high would you rank on job satisfaction?

I heard a story about John D. Rockefeller that made it obvious why he amassed such a great fortune. He was absolutely fascinated with every aspect of his work — down to the smallest detail.

One afternoon he borrowed a dime from his secretary and commented, "Be sure to remind me of this transaction."

"Oh, that's nothing, Mr. Rockefeller," replied the secretary.

"Nothing!" exclaimed Rockefeller, "Why, that's two whole year's interest on a dollar!"

He placed an uncommon value on everything in life — from the million dollar transaction to the interest on a dime.

Should I Stay or Go?

It is easy to agree with Kahlil Gibran, who wrote, "If you cannot work with love but only with distaste, it is better that you should leave your work."

Is quitting your job the only answer? No. Before taking action that extreme, perhaps there is another question you should ponder:

"Is it possible that I could learn to love what I am currently doing?"

When I was a teenager I hated yard work — especially mowing the lawn. I'd look for any excuse to avoid the chore.

Several years later, when my wife and I bought our first

home, something happened to change my attitude completely. I was in the sports department of a clothing store and bought an item called a pedometer. It measures the distance you walk.

The next Saturday, when I mowed my lawn I decided to give the new gadget a try. I was shocked when I discovered that I walked just over three miles behind my lawn mower that afternoon.

From that moment forward I had a totally new outlook on yard work that has lasted until this day. I actually look forward to my weekly "workout." It is part of my exercise program.

When someone suggested that I buy a riding mower I responded, "No way!"

An Agent of Change

Recently in Pennsylvania, a man told me about the experience he had working in an atmosphere that brought him to the brink of mental collapse. "I hated everything about my boss — his condescending attitude, his foul language, his constant criticism of my work."

The man continued, "I got to the place where I even hated my co-workers. He said, "When Monday morning came, I would literally break out in a cold sweat driving to the office."

Fortunately, something happened to drastically change the situation. He told me, "A speaker who was visiting our church said something that hit me like a bullet. It was, 'Don't look at the world as a mine field, see it as a mission field. See yourself as an agent of change.'"

The man began entering his workplace as a brand new person. His boss and his fellow workers were no longer people he despised, they had now become challenges. "I couldn't wait to get to work to see how many lives I could change for the better," he exclaimed.

It worked. The stress disappeared and within two months his boss actually became his friend.

When we change, our environment changes too. We may even reach the place where we think like the great inventor, Thomas Edison, who declared, "I never did a day's work in my life. It was all fun."

It is time to accept the advice of the seven dwarfs who sang: "Whistle while you work!"

21

The Lamp that Never Fails

"The vitality of thought is
an adventure. Ideas won't keep!
Something must be done about them."
— Alfred North Whitehead

In Detroit I once took a tour of a large General Motors plant that covered several acres and employed thousands of workers. Cars were coming off the assembly line and the sound of machinery was almost deafening.

As we walked between two large facilities I noticed a small building with several signs posted that read, "Danger. Keep Out!"

"What happens in that building?" I asked the guide.

"Oh, that is the most important structure on this property. It's the power plant. If that equipment were to shut down the entire operation would come to a standstill.

What is true at General Motors also applies to you. There is a small power plant inside each of us with an "On" and

"Off" switch attached. It can light up your life faster than any computer.

What is the secret source of power? It is an energy called expectation. It can be triggered by one simple thought that can instantly transform our behavior.

- We think about biting into a juicy hamburger and suddenly we find ourselves headed for the nearest Burger King.
- The very thought of being with someone we love can keep us wide awake in the middle of the night.
- We envision traveling to a distant location and begin to tingle with excitement.
- We smell a fresh pot of coffee and are stimulated before we even drink it.

Those are the positive examples. Negative expectations can also have a profound impact on our system.

- We hear footsteps behind us on a dark street and our heart begins to pound.
- We see a black spider in the corner of the room and want to run for the nearest door.
- We hear the sound of a gunshot and are frozen with terror.
- An automobile suddenly swerves toward the middle of the road and we nervously grip the steering wheel.

Energy Indicators

The mind-body link is too well documented to be ignored.

For example, studies have shown that fatigue is not as much a physical problem as a mental one. Many people are tired because they *want* to be tired. As one psychologist put it, "What people are trying to do when they complain of being tired all the time is to find a way to escape from life with dignity — with no criticism of their behavior."

Perhaps they are tired because they are facing a problem too big for them to solve.

What is the solution for this kind of fatigue?

Is it vitamins? Is it diet? Is it rest?

No. A simple dose of positive anticipation will release more energy than any pill.

On the dashboard of your car is a small indicator with a plus (+) and a minus (-) sign. That tells you if power is flowing to your alternator. If your battery is being drained, you won't be traveling much farther.

Negative thoughts act in much the same way. They pull your energy to them like a vacuum and leave you running on empty.

One thing is certain, your thoughts cannot be both positive and negative at the same time. One force will always dominate. It is like a wrestling match between the forces of good and evil.

How can we tap a fresh source of strength? Just one small spark from an idea and our stamina and vitality is miraculously renewed.

My Feet are Killing Me!

Often, when my wife has traveled with me to a city where I am scheduled to speak, she will choose to spend her time at a shopping mall rather than at my seminar. Once, when I picked her up at the appointed time she complained, "I thought 5:30 would never come. My feet are killing me!"

About a week later the routine was repeated in another city, but when I arrived to meet her, she wasn't there. I parked the car and walked though the mall until I spotted her. She looked at her watch and exclaimed, "Oh, is it that time already? I could have shopped for hours!"

I realize that women can often defy explanation but I finally figured out why she can be full of energy one day and exhausted the next. Here it is. When she is broke her feet begin to hurt, but when she has money, she is a non-stop shopper!

A Fourth Wind?

Those who have run the Boston Marathon or have competed in the bicycle race, Tour de France, will tell you what it feels like to get your "second wind" during one of these grueling events.

Harvard psychologist, William James, said, "If an unusual necessity forces us onward, a surprising thing occurs. The fatigue gets worse up to a certain point, when, gradually or suddenly, it passes away and we are fresher than before!" He says, "We have evidently tapped a new level of energy."

James explained, "There may be layer after layer of this experience, a third and fourth 'wind.' We find amounts of ease and power that we never dreamed ourselves to own, sources of strength habitually not taxed, because habitually we never push through the obstruction of fatigue."

The Four "C's"

When a chemist mixes certain ingredients, the combined formula is often more powerful than the sum of the individual parts. The same phenomenon occurs when we connect our mind, our will and our emotions.

Positive expectation combined with a strong belief produces more than hope; it creates confidence.

Walt Disney once said, "Somehow I can't believe that there are any heights that can't be scaled by a man who knows the secret of making dreams come true. This special secret, it seems to me, can be summarized in four C's." What was Disney referring to? The four "C's" are:

1. *Curiosity* — Having an inquisitive nature that raises new questions and searches for answers.
2. *Confidence* — A personal expectation that what you believe you will surely receive.
3. *Courage* — A bold spirit of adventure that moves every barrier in its path.
4. *Constancy* — The ability to move steadily forward regardless of the detours or distractions.

Looking at the list, Disney said, "The greatest of these is confidence. When you believe in a thing, believe in it all the way, implicitly and unquestionably."

Your Next Stop

What good things do you want to happen in the next few months? Don't just think about them. Write them down and start believing they will transpire.

What we expect become self-fulfilling prophecies. In a process that is difficult to comprehend, our actions obey our desires like a trained animal obeys its master.

Some people spend their life in such a rut that the pages of their book of memories are blank. They live in a fog — oblivious to almost everything around them.

In New York I heard about a visitor who boarded a subway on Fifth Avenue. After he found a seat, he turned to the fellow next to him and asked, "Can you tell me the name of the next stop?"

"Sorry, I can't," the man replied. "I've been riding this line for fifteen years and I only know two stops. Where I get on and where I get off."

Today and Tomorrow

Since life is governed by habits, why not get hooked on

hope? Fill your thoughts, your prayers, and your conversation with such faith and belief that there is no longer room for doubt. It will cease to exist because there is nothing on which it can feed.

How will you know when hope and expectation are a permanent part of you life? It will be expressed in dozens of ways.

- In the morning, you will ask, "I wonder what great thing is going to happen today?"
- At noon, you will say, "Sure there are challenges, but I know I'll make it through!"
- At night, you will declare, "Lord, I'm turning things over to you. I know you'll take care of them until tomorrow."

22

A New You Everyday

"Why wish for the privilege of living your past life again? You begin a new one every morning."
— Robert Quillen

Don't live one more day trapped in the "I don't know what to do" syndrome. It will only increase your insecurity and fuel your fear.

Medical research has established that a prolonged state of anxiety and worry so affects the body that it sets the stage for almost every type of disease. It ravages the body's glandular and chemical balance and opens the floodgates to a sea of physical problems.

However, not all fears are bad. Many of them are wholesome — and necessary for life. They include:

- The fear of fire.
- The fear of electricity.
- The fear of weapons.
- The fear of God.

These are life-sustaining fears.

Often, those we expect to be confident will tremble in a crisis.

During World War II, a military official summoned General George Patton in Sicily. As he praised Patton for his courage and bravery, the General interrupted: "Sir, I am not a brave man — the truth is, I am an utter craven coward. I have never been within the sound of gunshot or in sight of battle in my whole life that I wasn't so scared that I had sweat in the palms of my hands."

He admitted his anxiety, but it did not alter his battlefield decisions. Years later, when George Patton's autobiography was published, it contained this significant statement: "I learned very early in my life never to take counsel of my fears."

A Two Word Solution

What is the basic remedy for fear? It begins by heeding a two-word command found in the Bible 365 times — once for every day of the year. The words are: "Fear not."

John Edmund Haggai, in his book *How to Win Over Worry*, says, "A friend told me of his mother who worried for forty years that she would die of cancer. She died at seventy-three — *from pneumonia!*"

Says Haggai, "Tragic! She wasted forty years worrying about the wrong thing. Forty years she brought depression instead of delight to the hearts of her closest friends and members of her family. Forty years she divided her mind and her time between useful pursuits and worrying about cancer."

We have a choice regarding how we will face each day.

We can either exist with constant fear and anxiety or we can choose to live with zest and enthusiasm.

It's a Skill

When most people see a bright, cheerful, outgoing extrovert they think, "It must be wonderful to be born with that disposition!"

Born happy? You must be kidding. It was a painful experience and we all entered this world screaming our lungs out!

Without doubt, those we see as optimistic extroverts made some early choices that affected their behavior. However, it is never too late for change.

I have met scores of people who have successfully traded their dull, boring personality for one that is filled with a spirit that is contagious. I can tell you with confidence that enthusiasm is an acquired skill. That is difficult for some people to believe, but it's true. You can master the art of being enthusiastic.

Behavioral researcher Shad Helmstetter, in his book, *Choice,* says, "When we meet someone who seems to have a good attitude about everything, that really isn't the case. That person simply has made a lot of independent choices to have a good attitude about many individual things."

Continues Helmstetter, "That personality we call our 'attitude' is nothing more (and nothing less) than the sum total of all the small, daily choices we make — or fail to make — about how we feel."

Before Zig Ziglar became an author and motivational speaker, he set records for a national sales company. How did he reach his goals? Through personal excitement that came to the surface with every presentation. In his book, *Secrets of Closing the Sale,* Ziglar states that, "For every sale you miss because you're too enthusiastic, you will miss a hundred because you're not enthusiastic enough."

The Power of an Idea

How can we tap into the spring from which the rivers of excitement flow? The great historian Arnold Toynbee wrote, "Enthusiasm can be aroused by two things; first, an idea which takes the imagination by storm; and second, a definite, intelligible plan for carrying that idea into action."

Those who choose to live with fervor instead of dullness are constantly looking for ways to do things that are new and different. I recently heard about a man who went to a business reception and wrote the words "Financial Planner" on his name tag. It seemed that no one looked twice.

He got a new tag and wrote "Money" under his name, and was suddenly approached by several people who asked, "What does that mean?" He found some new clients!

It Really Works

Pete Rose was asked what part of a baseball player wears out first — "His eyes, his legs, or his arms?" Rose responded, "None of those things are the first to go. It's when his enthusiasm goes that he's through as a player."

You may ask, "What's the use of being enthusiastic if you really are not?"

It is much like putting on a new piece of clothing or having your hair professionally styled. When we feel better about ourselves, our outlook changes.

William James, the Harvard psychologist, believed that we feel the way we act. Therefore, enthusiasm works like this:

If you are going to feel enthusiastic, you must be enthusiastic.

I'm not an advocate of living a phoney life, but why go through your days choosing pessimism and gloom?

The real passion for what you do, however, needs to come from deep inside. As Norman Vincent Peale said, "Throw your heart over the fence and the rest will follow."

Soul Food

Take the time to count your blessings along the way.

Many years ago, Elbert Hubbard wrote an essay called, *White Hyacinths*. It included these words: "If I had only had ten cents, I would spend half of it for a loaf of bread and the other half to buy white hyacinths to feed my soul."

There is nothing like peace of mind or a tranquil heart.

The popular poet, Rod McKuen, wrote, "I measure success by how well I sleep on a given night. If I don't have to question my motives for any particular action I might have undertaken, or knowingly caused another human being trouble or discomfort, then I am at peace with my God and myself and I fall asleep easily. If sleep comes hard, then I know the day has been a personal failure."

When you do what is right the words found in Isaiah 57 will spring to life: "You found renewal of your strength, and so you did not faint."

23

It's Time to Write your Will

"The difference between a successful person and others is not a lack of strength, not a lack of knowledge, but rather a lack of will."
— Vince Lombardi

Year after year people make "I should" plans. They say:

- I should stop being so negative.
- I should be more forgiving.
- I should set higher goals.
- I should make some new friends.
- I should make better use of my time.
- I should not be so fearful.
- I should stop feeling sorry for myself.
- I should be more enthusiastic.
- I should read my Bible more.

Why do many of those wishes fail to come true? It is because "I should" is a self-condemning phrase that contains no precise timetable, obligation or commitment.

no precise timetable, obligation or commitment.

Equally dangerous is the phrase, "You should." It is a commonly used expression, but if we are not careful it can be interpreted as a desire to control the behavior of others. "You should go back to college," or, "You should join Weight Watchers."

As quickly as possible, change your "I should" vocabulary to "I will."

Don't say, "I should be more forgiving," say, "I will be more forgiving."

If the great enterprises of the world see the necessity of being guided by a mission statement, so can we. Here are seven "wills" we can make.

1. I will change what others are not willing to change.

A century ago, even before the Wright brothers, many creative people were very close to inventing the airplane. Orville and Wilbur were using the same principles that were being used by others, but they added a new dimension. They attached movable flaps and developed the forerunner of the modern airplane.

Not only to beat our competition, but to become the person God intended, we need flaps that move and propellers that spin.

- Others are not willing to change their negative habits. What about you?
- Others are not willing to stop procrastinating. What about you?
- Others are not willing to end their bigotry. What about you?

2. I will live to my fullest potential.

As George Bernard Shaws's life was nearing its end, a reporter challenged him to play the "What if" game.

"Mr. Shaw," he began, "you have been around some of the most famous people in the world. You are on a first-name basis with royalty, world-renowned authors, artists, teachers, and dignitaries from every part of this continent." Then he was asked,

"If you had your life to live over and could be any-body you've ever known, who would you want to be?"

Shaw thought for a moment and replied, "Sir, I would choose to be the man George Bernard Shaw could have been but never was."

How would you answer the same question?

- Who is it you would choose to be like?
- What is it you want your life to become?

- If you had your life to live over, what different path would you take?

Striving to be like someone else or attempting to achieve what others have done is not the road to developing your true potential. God created you as a unique individual with gifts and talents all your own. Don't be a copy-cat or an imitation. Be you!

3. I will control what I can and not worry about the rest.

I continue to meet people who fret about things over which they have no authority or power.

- They worry about being struck by lightning.
- They worry about catching a cold or a virus.
- They worry about being hit by a drunk driver.
- They worry about becoming stressed, not realizing that stress can be caused by worry.

Common sense and logic tells us to stay inside during a storm, to take our vitamins and to buckle our seat belts. Then, when you have done all you can, clear your mind of anxiety.

At a marina in Miami I saw a plaque on which was inscribed these words:

You cannot control the wind but you can turn the sail.

4. I will never allow my dream to die.

In 1974, when Muhammad Ali knocked out George Foreman in the eighth round of their heavyweight fight in Zaire, the world thought Foreman's boxing days were over. But twenty years later, at the age of 45, George Foreman still had a dream. He shocked people around the globe when once again he became heavyweight champion of the world.

You are never too old to dream.

- A former school teacher from Milwaukee, Golda Meier, became the prime minister of Israel at the age of seventy.
- After retiring at the age of sixty-five, Harland Sanders started Kentucky Fried Chicken.
- The famous American primitive painter, Grandma Moses, started her career at the age of seventy-eight and continued her work until she was 101.

You may have weeks, months, and even years of interruptions on your voyage, but never abandon your dream or resign yourself to failure.

5. I will make steady progress every day.

When it comes to personal achievement, speed is not as important as steady progress.

One of your resolutions needs to be to do something — *anything* — that moves you a little closer toward your goal.

As a writer, I have a goal to write for a minimum of thirty minutes every day. What usually happens is that during the scheduled half hour I often become so inspired and enthused about my topic that I continue to write for an hour, or two, or ten and even longer.

6. I will recognize the source of my strength.

The Greek philosophers taught, "Know thyself"
The Romans leaders declared, "Rule thyself."
The Chinese teachers said, "Improve thyself."
But Christ said "Without me you can do nothing."

Instead of praying for God to give you strength, realize that He is your strength and power — all you will ever need.

If you have ever learned to float on the surface of the water you know what happens if you try with your own effort. It won't work. You will sink. But when you give yourself completely to the water you can feel it coming under you, lifting you up and holding you with its power. That is what God will do if you will let Him.

Cherish the promise of God written in the sixth chapter of Hebrews: "Never will I leave you; Never will I forsake you."

7. I will never look back.

"I would have won if I hadn't glanced over my shoulder to see who was behind me," said a college track star after barely losing the championship in the 100-meter run.

When you have made a decision to reach new heights, the past should be relegated to the history books. We need to heed the words of Jesus, who said, "No one having put his hand to the plow, and looking back, is fit for the kingdom of God."

Keep your eyes on the prize and say, "I will."

24

Now That You Know What to Do

"I will go anywhere
as long as it is forward."
— David Livingstone

One of my favorite stories in the Old Testament is that of a prophet by the name of Elijah. There was a showdown on Mount Carmel between the man of God and 450 prophets of Baal. They wanted to see who served the real God — one who could call fire down from heaven. You can read about it in the eighteenth chapter of First Kings.

They set up two special altars and placed the meat of an animal over sticks of wood on each, but didn't light the fire.

After the worshippers of Baal spent an entire morning trying to get a response from their god, Elijah began to taunt them. "Shout louder!" he said. "Perhaps he is deep in thought, or busy, or traveling. Maybe he is sleeping and must be awakened."

All afternoon they were in a frenzy, but nothing happened.

Finally it was Elijah's turn. On the altar he had prepared he asked the critics to fill four large jars with water and pour them on the wood. They did this three times until the water filled the trench around the sacrifice.

Then the prophet stood and prayed a simple prayer. "O Lord, God of Abraham, Isaac and Israel, let it be known today that I am your servant and have done all these things at your command."

What happened? The fire fell and the people were astonished.

It's Not Over!

That is not the end of the story.

Elijah made a big mistake. He became so excited over his victory that he had all 450 of Baal's prophets put to death. Well, when king Ahab heard what happened he was furious. He sent word to Elijah through Jezebel that he would be killed and the prophet ran for his life.

After an exhausting day's journey in the desert he sat under a juniper tree and prayed that he might die, "I have had enough, Lord," he cried. "Take my life; I am no better than my ancestors." Then he stretched out under the tree and fell asleep.

An angel came and touched him, saying, "Get up and eat!" There was some fresh bread and a jar of water. He took it and again went to sleep.

The angel came a second time and said, "Please eat again, for the journey is too great for you."

Elijah arose, and traveled forty days and nights to Mount Horeb.

Think of it! On the strength of that meal he walked one hundred and fifty miles through the desert and climbed a mountain.

Friend, you may have reached a point in your life where you want to give up. Remember this: No matter how bleak the future may seem, when God touches your life you've got more time. You have *more* than forty days and forty nights. The Lord says, "When you drink of the water I will give you, you will never thirst again!"

Don't give up. An angel is on the way to touch your life, to give you strength, to lead you through the valley, across the desert and up to the peak of the mountain.

It's not over!

Many Roads, One Goal

I believe as you have been digesting these pages your mind has been whirling with activity. Not only is your dream coming into focus, but you are establishing your objectives and designing your strategy. Even if "Plan A" doesn't work, go to plan "Plan B." It that approach fails, don't hesitate to try "Plan C."

The most important principle is that your dream and your goal never, never change. How you get there may be far different than you first envisioned, but the destination is still the same. For example, if you decide to journey from New

York City to Boston there are dozens of roads you can travel — expressways, short-cuts, and scenic routes down winding roads.

It is not necessary to be bound by a rigid set of rules. Take your cue from children. Have you ever noticed how kids create and re-create a game? The goal, however, does not change. It's "play time" and they want to enjoy themselves.

In a dynamic, ever changing world, look for new gateways that may suddenly appear.

Helen Keller, a woman who learned to achieve although she was both deaf and blind, said, "When one door of opportunity closes, another opens; but often we look so long at the closed door that we do not see the one which has been opened for us."

Three Ingredients

At the age of six, W. Clement Stone was fighting to survive on the streets of Chicago, peddling newspapers. Stone wrote, "Years later I used to think of that little boy, almost as if he were not me but some strange friend from long ago. Once, after I had made my fortune and was head of a large insurance empire, I analyzed that boy's actions in the light of what I had learned." Stone concluded that there were three necessary ingredients for success.

> ***One: Inspiration to action*** — that which motivates you to act because you want to.

Two: Know-how — the particular techniques and skills that consistently get results for you when applied.
Three: Activity knowledge — knowledge of the activity, service, product, methods, techniques and skills with which you are concerned.

Stone believes these can be acquired by anyone, regardless of his current environment, age, color, occupation or education. "Success," he explained, "is achieved by those who try and keep trying."

Do you remember the story of Job? He endured great affliction during his walk through the valley, but never wavered in his faith. Job declared:

"What you decide on will be done, and light will shine on your ways."

Five Life-Changing Words

"Neil, we have a speaker coming to our annual awards banquet I thought you might like to hear" said a friend who worked for a life insurance company.

"Who is it?" I asked.

"Have you ever heard of Napoleon Hill?" he inquired.

"Heard of him? Of course! I have read his book, *Think and Grow Rich,* a dozen times."

On a Saturday evening, my wife and I were his guests at the event in the ballroom of a local hotel.

Napoleon Hill, who passed away not long after that time, was in rare form. He gave an enthusiastic address and received several standing ovations.

Following his speech, I made my way to the front of the room to shake his hand. After waiting while he conversed with a large number of well-wishers, I finally introduced myself and told him how much I enjoyed his presentation.

He brushed my praise aside and surprised me by asking this question: "What do you do?" he wanted to know.

When I told him, he said five words I have thought about many times since that moment. Hill grasped my hand tightly, looked me straight in the eyes and said:

"Give it all you've got!"
He repeated the words again.
"Give it all you've got!"

The next morning, as I was about to rise for the day, I mulled over those words. They greatly encouraged me. I didn't just slowly roll out of bed. I jumped up, walked to the nearest mirror, looked myself in the face and repeated the words out loud, "Give it all you've got!"

Many years have passed and that simple statement continues to inspire me to action.

Do It!

In the time it has taken you to read this book, I believe you have already traveled a great distance from where you started. Your dreams are closer, your goals are clearer, and your plans are more concrete.

I also believe you have a new sense of confidence and commitment that the direction you have chosen is not only your will, but also God's will for your life.

On your path there will no doubt be times of joy and moments of sorrow, but think about these words penned by William James: "I don't sing because I'm happy. I'm happy because I sing."

Now that you know what to do — *Do It!*

To schedule the author as guest speaker contact:

Neil Eskelin
Box 472812
Charlotte, NC 28247

FAX (704) 846-8965